Dr. Patti Giebink's *Unexpected Ch[...]* captivating, inspiring, and eloque[...] a long time. As a former abortion[...] qualified to speak to the topic mo[...] about. It's a deeply personal journey that sheds light on both sides of the abortion issue. Every teenager and adult will find invaluable guidance within its pages. I laughed. I lamented. I learned. But most of all, I praised God's grace!

DAVID STEVENS, MD, MA (ETHICS)
CEO emeritus of the Christian Medical & Dental Associations
Author of *Jesus, MD, Beyond Medicine*; coauthor of *Leadership Proverbs*

During my early years at Live Action, I dreamed of people like Patti stepping away from the abortion industry. Now, in *Unexpected Choice*, we are privileged to read the heart-wrenching and beautiful real-life story of transformation, from abortion clinic worker to pro-life advocate. The world needs more women like Patti. I pray that this book will inspire a new generation to follow her example of leaving the abortion industry and redeeming lost years by sharing a message of life. If you've picked up this book, there's a reason you've been led to it. Buy it now and never look back.

LILA ROSE
President and founder, Live Action

One of the greatest moments of ministry in my life was when our dear friend Patti Giebink stood before 70,000 people at The Call Nashville and began to confess and weep about her experience as a former abortion doctor. The crowd began to chant, "We love you! We love you!" I felt at that moment that God gave America ten more years of mercy. Now, we get to hear her compassionate and loving heart and story in this book. It's a story of redemption and forgiveness which we all so desperately need. "Patti, we love you!"

LOU ENGLE
Lou Engle Ministries

As an OBGYN colleague, I have the highest respect for Dr. Patti Giebink and her dedication to women's health. *Unexpected Choice* chronicles her journey from abortion doctor to pro-life advocate and addresses important questions for anyone trying to understand what motivates most physicians who do perform abortions as well as those who don't. Patti's ability to deftly articulate both sides of this issue makes this book a must-read for all who want to understand the phenomenon of elective abortion. I highly recommend it.

DONNA J. HARRISON, MD
CEO, American Association of Pro-Life Obstetricians and
Gynecologists (AAPLOG); board-certified OB/GYN

Dr. Patti Giebink's motto while working as an abortionist for Planned Parenthood was "Keep women safe." She soon learned that what they wanted from her as a doctor was "two hands and no conscience." But through the prayers of a secret intercessor and an inspired visit to a church in her new town, she began to see God more clearly—as a lover of life. Dr. Giebink and coauthor Kimberly Shumate have joined the battle for the hearts and minds of those still blind to the truth—that abortion hurts women. In my own work with former abortionists, I have seen the power and beauty of these journeys. In the book *Unexpected Choice: An Abortion Doctor's Journey to Pro-life*, you will see it as well.

FATHER FRANK PAVONE
National director of Priests for Life; president of the National Prolife Religious Council; pastoral director of Rachel's Vineyard

Unexpected Choice takes us on Patti's unfiltered journey from happy delivery room with parents celebrating their baby's birth, to the place where she performed abortions for Planned Parenthood. It's a transparent, gut-wrenching, and sometimes graphic account of the lucrative abortion industry with examples of disinformation commonly provided to pregnant women. It also debunks the myths used by abortion advocates while offering a compassionate look at the fear attached to unwanted pregnancy. Patti explains that using just a few different words when speaking to women facing a hard decision can empower them with an unexpected choice—life for a baby, and freedom from the guilt, shame, and grief that accompanies abortion.

DONALD THOMPSON, MD, MPH & TM
Former director of Global Health Outreach (GHO)

Unexpected Choice

Patti Giebink, MD

with Kimberly Shumate

UNEXPECTED

AN ABORTION DOCTOR'S JOURNEY TO PRO-LIFE

CHOICE

FOCUS
ON THE FAMILY.

A Focus on the Family Resource
Published by Tyndale House Publishers

CONTENTS

Introduction *1*

CHAPTER 1: *Coming Clean 5*

CHAPTER 2: *From Invisible to Indelible 17*

CHAPTER 3: *The Septic Tank 33*

CHAPTER 4: *If They Could See through My Eyes 49*

CHAPTER 5: *It's Complicated 61*

CHAPTER 6: *Overseas Interlude 73*

CHAPTER 7: *The Prayer of Sister Josita 89*

CHAPTER 8: *Just Like Me 99*

CHAPTER 9: *It's a Prayer Meeting, Not a Protest 111*

CHAPTER 10: *Fan Mail to a Feminazi 125*

CHAPTER 11: *A Unique Human Being 141*

CHAPTER 12: *Myths, Risks, and One Last Kiss 155*

CHAPTER 13: *What Might Have Been 173*

CHAPTER 14: *In Solidarity of Life 185*

Acknowledgments *193*

Notes *195*

INTRODUCTION

LOVE. YOU MIGHT SAY IT'S WHY YOU and I are here—living, striving, dreaming. It was love that moved God to put us here. And though God's compassion is beyond our ability to comprehend, His reason for making us is simple. *Love.*

Unlike our love that can so easily change, God's love remains strong and steady, overflowing like a river that refuses to run dry. He is the unending source of life that watered the seed of creation. His love made us; therefore, we are irrevocably part of it. We search for it. Look past it. Deny it ever was. Yet, it still *is.*

God loves us so much that He uses others in conjunction with seemingly serendipitous circumstances to bring us closer to Him—always closer. And that is what God has done with me in my journey from performing abortions as part of my career as a doctor to eventually changing my viewpoint about life.

My life has been one of determined purpose, and my passion has always been caring for others. My youth and young adulthood were spent in classrooms, lecture halls, and residency to practice medicine. I was a teacher, a fitness specialist, and finally a physician committed to saving lives and doing no harm—an oath I promised to keep. My father was a doctor as well as two of my siblings. Health care was in my blood, and it led me to serve around the globe in countries such as India, Cambodia, Pakistan, Afghanistan, Lebanon, and the Arabian Peninsula. I've lived in dusty camps, sweltering villages, armed-guard compounds, and third-world hotels. Each place held new adventures, unique experiences, and disturbing images often at the doorstep of someone else's life and death.

But my years at home in the US introduced me to people who broadened my perspective even further. It was in a little church in South Dakota where God revealed my own faults and inadequacies and equipped me for a plan greater than my own expectations could have prepared me for.

Education, medical practice, professional ethics, personal morals, *faith*—they are all related. At least they are to me. And the tough topic of abortion intertwines with all of these subjects. Abortion is hard to talk about; it divides families and friends, and it's emotional, just as the journey we're about to travel together will undoubtedly be. I'm certain reading this book will be challenging for some of you. But sometimes the difficult roads help us look back and see the mistakes we've made as well as a new way to move forward—in the flesh and in the spirit.

In 1996, as the only abortion doctor in South Dakota, moving forward in my day usually meant putting on a bulletproof vest each morning and packing a sidearm before I headed to work. It meant I was part of an "active case" file with the FBI due to hate mail, the target of inflammatory messages on picket signs outside the clinic, and the recipient of death threats from people I had never met.

But when it comes to abortion, *is* there a safe way to move forward? I'm not only talking about physical safety, but also emotional, mental, and spiritual safety. Are there instances when abortion is acceptable, even medically beneficial? Or is every life—no matter how small or compromised—unconditionally viable and valuable? I'll let you decide. I only ask that you keep an open mind as we traverse the troubling and sometimes devastating landscape of the human condition.

It's fascinating the lengths our mind and memory will go to protect us. We can block out the past in order to cope in the present. But God reveals truth gently, sometimes incrementally, for us to look at, digest, and finally come to terms with it. This story is part of the truth that God gently led me to, and it's something I've suppressed for years. But I know *now* is the time to tell it.

Along the way, I've learned that redemption comes with God's gift of healing. Redemption is the reason for writing this book. As a former abortion doctor, I can't help but determine that my past had a black mark before meeting Jesus. It was lived and recorded and can't be reversed. But Christ's forgiveness covers all of it.

My history isn't remarkable: I'm only one of thousands of doctors who have performed abortions. In retrospect, the truly remarkable thing is that God was there with me through it all, even though I didn't always know it. His stubborn affection for me was never determined by my ability to be perfect. His forgiveness wasn't dependent on my questionable decisions and flawed execution. His awesome grace never hinged on my aptitude as a doctor or my willingness to do what seemed right at the time. God's redemption never winced, scowled in disgust, or turned its back on me. In the shadow of what I have done—as unthinkable as it is—God himself is "guilty" of an undeniable action: He loved me too much to let go.

And He loves you in that same way, as He loves all life. Love—it's who God is.

As a doctor who has seen more suffering than I ever thought I would; as one who has lived on both sides of this difficult abortion divide and spent years transitioning from one camp to the other, my prayer is that you'll discover the same reconciliation and peace that I've found. I pray that love prevails in your life and that my own unexpected choice will help you see life clearly—as I do now.

CHAPTER ONE

COMING CLEAN

The awareness of our own depravity is the root of perpetual tenderness.

JOHN NEWTON

I WAS IN MY BODY—I ASSUMED IT WAS MY BODY. Those were my feet; my legs were striding in a way I recognized. My arms swung in a synchronized fashion. But my body felt so alien and altogether stolen as it carried me in a direction I didn't want to go.

Was it the lack of sleep the night before that had set my stomach churning? Maybe it was the rush of chilly air from the vents of the convention hall now swirling over me, or the runny morning omelet that produced this ill feeling.

I dodged clustered tables filled with glowing faces. Here on the last day of a Christian conference I had driven six hours to attend, I was expecting to feel reflective, grateful, and maybe even a little reluctant for it to end. But terrified?

I admit that the prayer and biblical teachings still had

a foreign feel to them, a mysterious and illusive quality that I hadn't completely figured out. How did an analytical physician accustomed to proven conventional therapies end up here?

As a doctor, my decisions and actions were solely based on test results, tangible evidence, reason, and resource. Now the emotional atmosphere of this human "hug-fest" carried with it a strange sense of dread. Even fear. *Or is this what freedom feels like?*

My mind pleaded with my legs to stop, to turn around and return to my seat. But they kept walking straight ahead as the keynote speaker invited attendees to come on stage and share their thoughts in that final hour. Invisible arms gently guided me through the throng of tables, ushering me toward a frightening fate—to speak publicly, and about what, I wasn't even sure.

My thoughts suddenly drifted back home to a Christian coworker at the medical practice I shared at the Mid-Dakota Hospital located in Chamberlain, South Dakota. She was a fellow female OB-GYN who happened to be Catholic and pro-life. Her faith was unshakable, her convictions the foundation of her behavior and decisions. This made an indelible impression on me. She wasn't intimidating or pious, just enviable.

What must it be like to have such faith that it shapes every choice you make, whether favored by all or none?

On more than one occasion, I'd noticed her bravery as she voiced her opinion about life to colleagues during meetings and work-related groups. Her unwavering belief that life began from the moment of conception never seemed to be influenced by peer pressure or the popular vote. She was fixed on where the line was drawn in the sand, and in the years I watched her, she never did cross it. Not once.

As I walked through the crowd on my way to the stage, I couldn't help but think she would be much better suited to make a proclamation of faith—if that's what this invisible force was leading me to do. I had been attending a little church since 2001, slowly finding my way to a God who was becoming more evident with every demonstration of His grace. With one foot still in the world, I was unsteady and sometimes unnerved by what He was doing in and around me.

Now it was May 2006, and I'd traveled with a couple of friends from Chamberlain to Minneapolis for this five-day Christian conference focused on healing and deliverance. The conference appealed to me: I truly wanted to help those who trusted me for treatment, and I was willing to explore new ideas. Judith was an elementary teacher, and Susan was a gifted lay leader from our church who'd invited us to the event. We'd climbed into the car to leave Chamberlain just as the sky gave off hints of morning with its pink-crusted edges. We were filled with excitement for what would certainly be a time of fun and fellowship.

The endless drive crossed much of the flat South Dakota prairie, and we didn't reach the metro area until the last hour of the trip. Ignoring the gratingly synthetic tone of the "GPS lady," I circumvented the busy downtown Minneapolis traffic, arriving on schedule for the conference's 1:00 p.m. start time.

Standing in front of the large church with hundreds of

other people attending the convention, I craned my neck upward to take in the building. Suddenly, I felt much smaller. And as we found our seats amid the great assembly, I surveyed the crowd. A symphony of handshakes, hugs, and introductions filled the air about me. People from various backgrounds were all eager to begin the workshops offered by Ellel Ministries International, a nondenominational ministry established and based near Lancaster, England. The founder, Peter Horrobin, was known worldwide and a respected leader in the religious community. What gems of wisdom or remarkable remedies would I discover worth taking back to my own practice? How did prayer affect healing, and could I apply it to the care of my own patients?

I was open and engaged. More than I knew.

After the afternoon's orientation, my friends and I checked into our hotel located close to the church. The next four days we listened to lectures and made new friends among diverse faith-filled men and women.

I could have applied the word *blessing* to those four days, though at the time that word was not a description I often used—I probably used the words *lucky* or *fortunate* more often. But it was a *blessing* to be in the midst of such uncompromising believers and absorbing the Holy Spirit, who was so present throughout the entire week. I felt full— in my mind and in my heart.

I was content, except for an unrelenting uneasiness that kept one hand gripping the chair I sat in. Images surfaced of the past weeks, months, years—a photo album of personal and professional memories of my previous life. And I was uncomfortable with what I saw.

In the process of remembrance, our mental pictures change as we change. They are liquid, moving, dispatching then rebuilding as we gain more knowledge. The way we view our lives is like a novel with shifting plots and subplots, where villains and heroes switch places, protagonists make hurtful choices, and antagonists find redemption by the final chapter. In my own mental storybook of decisions and practices, where was my line in the sand?

Was God rewriting me?

On this last day of the conference as Judith, Susan, and I were swapping conversations with new acquaintances, Peter invited attendees to come up to the stage and briefly talk about their experiences over the previous several days. Those with more willing souls than mine immediately formed a line, eagerly waiting their turn to share reflections about what they had learned. Revelations about God and prayers answered reverberated from the sound system.

I sat listening with my own sense of gratitude kindled by a deep warmth that took me somewhat off guard. It was like someone was speaking to me on a frequency only I could hear. No, *feel*. It was a feeling, but it spoke to me with an uneasy prodding as the line to the stage steadily grew.

What was it telling me to do? I knew I couldn't be hearing it right.

In general, I rarely spoke up in large groups. The fact was, I would sooner die than verbally address that packed room of faithful believers.

But as I sat rigid in my seat, I felt a cosmic shove—a not-so-subtle invitation to join in. My hands began to sweat, and my lungs seized as I stood up and started walking. Nausea hit me as I took my place—the last one in the line.

"We're running out of time, so we'll hear the testimonies of the last few before we wrap things up," Peter announced. Now I was helplessly stuck, a prisoner of God's almighty persuasion. Just then, a calmness embraced me like an old friend—a friend who's always been there and always will be, who would do anything for you, even if you were exiled due to public disgrace. This friend would shield you from the stress of the most disturbing development—and that's what was happening right then.

Since I was in clear view of the entire assembly, it seemed I was committed. Did I even know what I was going to say, or did the Influencer commandeering my trembling limbs have something of His own to impart?

The stage, the twenty or so tables that held eight to ten people each, the volunteers buzzing around—it all looked like a dream, kind of fuzzy and out of focus. I had met so many people who traveled from all over to be there, just as I had. But I felt certain that even those experts of kindness and mercy surrounding me must have their limits.

Suddenly, there were only two of us left in line. The woman ahead of me floated up the stairs confidently, then rested one hand on the microphone. She said she was a nurse in an operating room. My ears burned. With luck, the building would catch fire and the crowd would run.

Until then, no one had mentioned the A-word. All I wanted to do was sprint for the nearest exit. I tried to turn, to flee, but my invisible Friend kept hold of my hand as we stayed the troubled course.

God, please don't do this!

No one knew my story. I hadn't even thought about it . . . until now.

The Bible says that Jesus wants to heal us. "He was pierced for our transgressions; he was crushed for our iniquities . . . and with his wounds we are healed" (Isaiah 53:5). But what would these godly people think if they knew what I had done? How could I just come out and say it?

The woman on stage spoke up.

"I'm a surgical nurse at St. Paul Ramsey Hospital," she said, sweetly. "One day, I noticed on my schedule that I would be assisting with an abortion. I went to my supervisor and told her that I couldn't do it, that it was against my morals. She basically said that I would assist in the procedure or look for another job." Her eyes pooled with tears as she continued, "So, I looked for another job."

God, are you kidding? I can't do what You're asking me to do . . .

By now, I realized that God had orchestrated this from the beginning. Planned it. Perhaps He was even enjoying it. And I was powerless to stop it. Swaying slightly, I gathered myself to step out from behind the curtain—a beige façade of safe anonymity.

When the nurse finished her declaration—a statement of what scruples really looked like—she made her way back to the stairs, passing me as I was half laughing and half crying. My polished veneer was about to lose its attractiveness. I wanted to keep my dark secret. To hide and pretend that I hadn't done anything wrong. And until that moment, I had convinced myself I was guilt free by simply not thinking about my past. But to be truly healed and set free of something, you have to expose it to the light.

Because freedom lives in the light.

Peter's friendly wave reeled me up the stairs and onto the platform. I was less than brave—just reluctantly obedient. I looked out at all those faces, beaming with the glow of God's light. Three hundred and fifty people waited in anticipation as I thought for a minute I might actually pass out.

With one painful shudder and a sob that quickly followed, my eyes lowered and my mouth opened as if God Himself was speaking through me, forcing me to deal with my past. I don't think I said I was a doctor, or where I practiced. Not even my name. Just the depressing point I could no longer escape.

"I'm proof that God can redeem anyone. I used to perform abortions for Planned Parenthood." Then the tears rained down.

After a collective gasp, the room fell quiet. I could only imagine everyone trying to absorb what they had just heard.

There it was. The fatal shot. My hands had squeezed the lethal trigger. Unlike that surgical nurse, I saw things differently—at least I had until then. A tiny life nestled within a woman's womb was just a small collection of tissue, void of sensation, and nothing more. Not seeing. Not feeling. Not breathing.

Not human.

This unplanned confession left me feeling overwhelmed and ashamed. The conference-goers must have been horrified at what I had done! And so I left my gaze resting on the floor. Unexpectedly, I felt Peter Horrobin's arms wrapping me in an all-consuming, all-forgiving, Father-God hug as I broke down completely.

God, forgive me. If You can, just forgive me.

Afterward, women walked up to me and held me, as if to soothe my sorrow with a balm of understanding. Some revealed that they'd had an abortion. To my surprise, we shared the same pain, guilt, sadness, isolation, and fear of others discovering our offense. They thanked me for speaking out, for talking about a subject so taboo that it's rarely discussed from the pulpit.

Instead of condemnation—the judgment I expected—all I received from these people was overpowering love.

How could this be—love for someone like me?

Yes, I wanted to grow my faith. Yes, I'd traveled all that way to expand my point of view and to learn how prayer and healing related to my job. That's what I had in mind. But God seems to always reach further than our own expectations. He knows the way, the challenges, the fear, and the outcome. All we are required to do is trust and show up.

That afternoon, the drive home was spent ignoring the "elephant" in the car. Judith and Susan were generous that way. Weird how my confession carried with it a pact of non-disclosure. But what can you really say about abortion? It's so offensive to some, so sensible to others. For a long time, I had neatly tucked my involvement with it into the back of my brain, disregarding it, trying to forget it. And that's what

I did again when I got home from that conference. If only God's memory was as short as mine.

I didn't tell anyone back at my little church in Chamberlain about what I'd said in Minneapolis, or what I was internally coping with. That would come later.

Looking back, I have no regrets about coming clean. Yes, it was painful, but it was also freeing. I had finally exhaled that toxic breath inside of me, and now it was out, all the way out, leaving room for God's holy oxygen to fill me with forgiveness, for myself and for others.

I suspect we've all had, at some point, a crisis in our faith walk when God convicts us of something we're hanging on to—whether for days, years, or decades. God might point to a habit, a lifestyle, anger, or a grudge. By a test of our conscience or a circumstance beyond our control, God reveals it to us, guides us to remorse and admission, and then His forgiveness enables us to heal and move forward. The conviction of what I'd done, and the divine amnesty that followed gave birth to a ministry God had prepared for me well in advance.

Who can say how many plans in the grand design have been squandered because of our fear to trust God or our pride that says we know best? How many wounds have we incurred and injuries have we inflicted due to our short-sightedness as we fail to see things from a higher perspective? What is the final cost of our self-significance, and who pays the price for it?

I believe that hurting people can be miraculously healed. And I trust that seeking Jesus for healing can only benefit the person asking the Great Physician—the One who makes us clean.

A SAFE PLACE TO PONDER

"[Jesus'] way is in whirlwind and storm,
and the clouds are the dust of his feet."

NAHUM 1:3

Lord,

*You said that in this world there will be trouble (John 16:33).
But You understand that being human is hard, and that we all
make mistakes. Thank You for overcoming the world and for
supplying all the grace we need to heal from our past. I know
that You are the Great Physician, and that Your remedies cover
a multitude of sins—too many to count. Place in me a spirit of
forgiveness—for myself, for those who have yet to confess their
secrets, and for those You will heal through my transparency.*

In Jesus' name, amen.

CHAPTER TWO

FROM INVISIBLE TO INDELIBLE

Faith walks simply, childlike, between the darkness
of human life and the hope of what is to come.

CATHERINE DOHERTY

THE SILENCE FRIGHTENED ME AS I wandered from room to room, searching for a sign of life. All the usual sounds, smells, running, talking, fighting, laughing, parents, brothers, sisters—*gone*. My cries disappeared into a noiseless vacuum. Tears, sobs, pleas—nothing brought them back.

How could they have forgotten me?

The panic and pain of that day ingrained itself into that four-year-old little girl casually left behind at home. After being all alone that day, I knew I was incredibly good at one thing. It wasn't a superpower or a gift. Just a trait I didn't want: I was invisible. And what could be worse for a child than feeling invisible?

On that terrifying day when I helplessly roamed the house, I found no one but my dolls and their tiny clothes that needed packing, as I decided it was better to run away than to stay in a place where I didn't matter. With my little suitcase in hand, I opened the front door and stepped outside.

It turned out that everyone had gone for ice cream and left me at home by mistake. They found me sitting on that doorstep with tearstained cheeks, clutching my suitcase and dolls. While I've come to terms with the feeling of helplessness I experienced that day, I've never forgotten how empty a child's life can be without love—the kind of love that sees everything.

In an era of station wagons, family dogs named Champ, and neighborhood houses designated as kid catchalls for children who ran and played until the sun went down, it was a chaotic yet consistent upbringing. There were no computers, cell phones, flat screens, or PlayStations. You climbed the trees in the yard next door and walked a few blocks to the convenience store to get a bottle of pop. And you read. Reading was a focal point in my family, and it occupied hours of my time.

With seven children in all (one with special needs), our house was a hive of activity. But at the end of the school year when the mercury started to rise, we escaped to the lake in Iowa. All the other kids in town never went anywhere. They were forced to suffer through three long months of boredom. But not us. We swam, sailed, hiked, and canoed all summer long. Dad was on call at the hospital, but he would join us on the weekends and a day or two during the week if his schedule permitted.

I was fifteen years old in 1965, when things were changing for girls and women all over the country. As the "invisible" middle child, I struggled to find my identity in a home filled with personalities vying for a spot in the family pecking order. That's when my Aunt Scottie told me about the Minnesota Outward Bound School, the first women's outdoor education course in the US. The opportunity to spend an entire month with more than twenty other young women out in the rugged wilderness of woods and lakes excited me. After all, I loved the outdoors life during those summers in Iowa.

At the time, no one thought women could exert themselves physically as they do today. It was a progressive yet unthinkable notion to take a bunch of females out into the wilderness by themselves to camp, explore, and test their mettle. This was a risky experiment and had never been tried before in the United States.

After my hard-fought campaign, Mom and Dad agreed to let me go. I filled out the application, included a check for $250 courtesy of Aunt Scottie, and sent it in. I could almost feel my independence staking its claim. There were no wallflowers within the pages of the *National Geographic*. Only daring explorers. That was me!

Our base camp was centralized, but our supervisors sent us out into the back territory for much of the month. Reflecting the sexism of the times, a couple of male shadows followed us as a safety precaution. The consensus in that time was that women simply weren't capable of taking care of themselves.

In addition to our daily activities, each girl would be

sent out on a three-day solo nature experience. With my background and love of the outdoors, I felt right at home in the remote terrain, pushing boundaries and stepping outside of the comfortable predictable norm. How could I have known my future was being shaped by every step I took?

A few months after we returned home, my picture appeared in *Seventeen* magazine and *Sports Illustrated*. Our success was such a novelty, it made some waves as well as opened up new opportunities for other young women. Unbelievably, I had made a noticeable difference.

My perspective of life and attitude about myself had been drastically altered. I was more confident and self-sufficient than ever before. Somehow, the improved inner identity didn't translate into finding my "tribe" at school, though I did spend a year on the cheerleading team. But there was someone I *did* notice, and he noticed me.

I think it was our mutual love of adventure and the outdoors that attracted us to each other. He and I climbed local rocks and peaks and went to the mountains at every opportunity. At long last, I was no longer forgotten, misplaced, or overlooked. Those early lessons in self-esteem provided me with the strength to move into young adulthood.

From my dear parents, I learned a few treasured things: to value truth and honesty, to stand behind your work, and to always do what you say you're going to do. They taught me that people are equal, and to never judge someone's outer appearance. I learned to have a heart for those less fortunate, to give whenever you can, and to always keep learning and growing.

And I learned plenty during my first semester at the University of Montana (a distance from my high school flame), where I studied wildlife biology and lived in the women's freshman dorm. The sheer size of the school was intimidating, but it also provided a new lens that sharpened my social awareness and interpersonal skills. In the midst of so many interesting people and ambitions, I was learning that the world was full of endless possibilities. At the end of my one and only semester at U of M, I moved back home to be with my boyfriend, since he was continually prodding me to return.

We were now both attending Augustana, a local liberal arts college in Sioux Falls, South Dakota. It didn't offer a wildlife biology program (my first choice was to work with animals), so I made do with physical education and sports studies. Between semesters, my man and I returned to scaling steep terrain, hiking many a rocky path, and embarking on our outdoor passions promising fresh air and a respectable workout.

In 1972, I graduated with a degree in physical education and a teaching certificate. Though my boyfriend and I met in tenth grade and kept the candle burning off and on throughout high school and college, by the time we tied the knot, the novelty of our romance had faded. We were simply doing what young couples did on their way to becoming full-fledged adults.

My parents never said anything for or against us getting married. But Mom made it clear that she wasn't in favor of a flashy extravaganza. Taffeta and flower arrangements weren't my style anyway, so she was appeased.

We said "I do" at the Baptist church I grew up in, an understated little chapel that fit our practical side. It was a tame affair. I think my dad walked me down the aisle, but I can't say for sure. And the fact that I can't remember only confirms how low-key it was. This meager nuptial ceremony with only family and friends didn't even offer a proper reception—just cake in the fellowship hall. I don't recall if there was even music, and I came away with about three photos of the event—one being us signing the license.

I taught for the first few years of our marriage, and we were happy. The pent-up energy of kids sequestered in classrooms and suddenly released for gym class was exhilarating, and working as a PE teacher, coach, and health instructor gave me a lot of joy. After teaching junior high, I returned to Montana for a master's degree in PE, which led me into fitness testing and exercise physiology. I spent most of the year in Bozeman without my husband since he was busy with his life in Sioux Falls. He eventually joined me at Christmas time and left again in the spring.

But there was an itch—an agitation, really—just below the surface that I thought could be quelled if we moved to Omaha, Nebraska, where he was offered a full-time management position. His schedule left me at home alone for hours on end. And since housekeeping wasn't exactly what I had pictured for a career, I started running long distance to fill up the vacant time.

As I met runners who taught me the finer points of long-distance racing, it seemed that my husband and I drifted further apart. But we were adolescent and selfish, and when our interests strayed from the original plan, there wasn't enough maturity to hold us together.

Following seven years of marriage, we divorced. Later I accepted an exercise physiologist job in California. My brother and his wife had already moved to San Francisco, and I stayed with them, close to where I worked at the old Presbyterian Hospital.

Scouring the ads for a neighborhood apartment, I quickly realized that the rents were well out of my price range. Everything I could afford was either in a gloomy basement or had the view of a brick wall. That's when someone told me I was going about it all wrong—that the affordable places worth living in would only be found on foot.

I set out one afternoon on Union Street, walking the hills parallel to the marina in search for just the right space. And there in the window of a lovely historic Victorian house was a "for rent" sign.

The owner's family lived on the main floor, and a female tenant occupied one of the two apartments on the second. The studio was perfect—bright, cheery, and a stone's throw from work. It had one enormous room with a high ceiling and bay windows facing east with the marina just out of view. After a quick climb to the roof, I could see the bay and the weather—a sun-kissed city or the fog rolling in. The apartment had no air conditioning, and it was heated only by a friendly fireplace that crackled on chilly days. This cozy nook not far from the bustle of streetcars and ferryboats became home—a respite of safety and support.

The change in scenery, as well as new friends and job duties, infused me with fresh excitement. My position at the Institute of Health Research didn't pay a lot, but I felt useful, like a different person in a story where I was suddenly the main character. At the very least, I was a woman who had a few compelling lines of dialogue, a bona fide three-dimensional heroine with a voice that continued to evolve.

Every day, I ran along the marina, taking in the flavorful sights and sounds, the hilly vistas that indulged my wandering notions, and the melting pot of humanity so unlike what I had grown up with. But with all of its unique and inspiring qualities, the Bay City's underbelly was dangerous, and several of my friends had violent encounters. It was something I hadn't dealt with before.

As a single woman having to constantly look over her shoulder and stay guarded at night, I suddenly heard the echo of a promise my siblings and I had made growing up: *Escape Sioux Falls, never to return!*

But did I really mean that?

Of course, a young person weighs her options on the scale of *never* and *forever*. But as we get older, never eventually becomes "later" and forever turns into "if things stay the same," leaving the door wide open for a change of heart. And though all of us did pack our bags and leave our hometown (excluding my sister with disabilities), we also came back one by one, save a single brother who decided *never* really *did* mean forever and ever, amen.

In 1980, I left San Francisco and headed home to Sioux Falls once more. Not only because of the big city dangers, but because of a strange conversation I had with my dad about returning to graduate school. In our family, education seemed to be the answer when considering the next move. But instead of the PhD I was considering, Dad suggested I go to medical school.

When I was young, I wondered who in their right mind would become a doctor. My dad labored nonstop and was always on call in the middle of the night, as well as during weekends and family outings. His time was never his own. He belonged to everyone in the community, and there his commitment stayed.

Suddenly, I was humoring the idea of becoming like my father (the overworked orthopedist), my cousin (the pediatrician), and my brother (the radiation oncologist). And the contamination didn't end there. My sister-in-law was a newly minted plastic surgeon, and my brother-in-law would end up becoming a gastroenterologist. Even my younger brother would eventually become a psychiatrist. I blame it solely on DNA. Doctoring is in our blood.

Yet medical school meant another four years of classrooms and hospital rotations, then an additional four years of residency.

If only life came with a defined path that you could follow from the very beginning! If only some all-knowing power designed a future specifically for you, one that led you to exactly where you were meant to be—your destiny.

No jumbled map, faulty compass, or impulsive headwind sent you in the wrong direction. No avalanches or dead ends got in your way. If only there was one wide, clearly marked hiking trail with a neon sign that read: "This is your future. Go straight and don't turn!"

But as time slowly reveals to us, even the byways—I won't call them mistakes—come with valuable experiences and insight that can influence and enrich us. Those detours are actually part of our destiny. Without them, who can say we'd be prepared for the future?

In 1981, I enrolled for prerequisites at Augustana College in Sioux Falls: organic chemistry, calculus, and physics (not so lovingly referred to as the "Mystery Hour"). You couldn't sleep through or phone in to these classes. At that point, I was thirty years old, and my classmates were smart, fast, young guns moving at the speed of light. In my attempt to dodge discouragement, I would sit in the corner during tests with my back to everyone, knowing I would be the last to finish. It's funny how the lesson in humility wasn't mentioned in the course description.

Thank goodness for my running buddy, Deirdre. A single girl like me, she was health conscious, fun loving, and had a dry sense of humor that made me giggle. Deirdre worked in a bank as she studied to become a financial planner.

Neither one of us really dated at the time. We just stayed busy running, working, and studying—until one day when she invited me to go swimming with her.

"Just think about it. The swim coach is really cute," she told me.

Deirdre was on the YMCA's adult swim team, and since

a nasty leg injury was keeping me out of my Nikes, I agreed to go along.

Michael was the swimming instructor and six years my junior—a mere pup of twenty-four. His girlfriend was stunning—very classy with a presence about her that reminded me of Jackie Onassis. The first time I saw them together, the two were sitting down to breakfast in a diner we all frequented. She was tall, her slender legs tucked beneath the table, and impeccably dressed.

I didn't know what she did for a living outside of attracting admiring glances. Each time I saw her it was from a distance, enabling my imagination to create the perfect woman.

As for Michael, like my ex-husband, he was handsome, charismatic, and fit. One big cliché of a prince.

I, on the other hand, wasn't much of a fashion plate, showing up at the YMCA in clodhopper boots, a pudgy down jacket, and dorky hat. It wasn't for lack of taste (I hope), but of interest. I just didn't care what I looked like, which was reflected in my archaic baggy swimsuit that was more like something old Aunt Betty would wear than a woman in her prime.

After class, my hair would freeze in the arctic bite as I walked home, which was of no concern since I was *not* looking for a boyfriend. My pre-entry classes for med school were demanding, and I had already ended a marriage. Still, Michael was undeniably adorable. But he was *taken*.

When my leg healed, I was glad to get back to running. Now it was spring. Spring! Sun, birds, trees reaching out to say hello with budding shoots of green. And since spring was a season that brought with it new beginnings, the question that Michael posed to me was somewhat appropriate for the theme.

"Mind if I come running with you sometime?"

Did I mention he was really cute? And he must have run in college because he wasn't slow. Even so, up hills, across town, and without mercy I ran him into the ground, proving I may have been Old Betty in the water, but I was no frump out of it.

Next came a request I thought for certain I had misheard.

"How about going out with me?"

What did he say? "I thought you had a girlfriend." *You know, your insanely exquisite, supermodel girlfriend.*

"Nope, I just broke up with her." That's all he said. And let's face it, that's all he needed to say.

"Sure, why not," I answered, still believing it was all very innocent. *What could Mr. Adonis possibly see in me?*

When I initially saw him across the diner with that gorgeous girl, I decided then and there that dating him wasn't an option. Suddenly, it was! The romance flew into overdrive, even though classes and working part-time at the VA hospital left me with little time to spare. But when you love someone (you heard me), especially a man who blindsides you the way Michael did me, you *make* time.

Spring drifted into a beautiful summer, and by winter, we were living together.

Michael and I moved out to the country along with his best friend. He and I ran through the crisp country air, cooked dinner together, and kissed in front of the glowing fire once our roommate had gone to bed. And when Michael found out my family owned a farm, he was positively elated.

"Patti, when we get married," Michael said excitedly, "let's go live there!"

Married?

The hippies that occupied the house built in the mid-1800s on the farm property had stopped paying rent—they were squatting—and had turned the place into an unsightly mess. Once they were out, the heavy renovations began. We replaced the drafty roof and some crusty siding, and covered it with a fresh coat of paint. Still, my mom wandered from room to room repeating, "You can't live here . . . you can't live here . . ."

She was right—it was a dump. But little by little, we fixed it up to a civilized standard. The home had just a wood-burning stove for heat and a rustic appeal only a hungry student could love. We raised Chesapeake Bay retrievers and had two horses, a small herd of cows, and crops of corn and alfalfa. Once again, I was steadily following my significant other's lead. Michael had quit his swimming coach position to become a farmer—a dream of his. *His.*

Still, I can't deny that it was a magical place, and that our time there together was sweet. Lightning bugs flickered against the purple and pink sunsets. There was a flirtatious reflecting pond, and a lovely little bridge that beckoned. The farmland itself rested against the picturesque Sioux River as tree branches languidly bent with the breeze that swept in from of the water's edge.

We chose this paradise and named it Autumn Creek's

Farm, our wedding site despite the ongoing repairs. About sixty well-wishers gathered in mid-August, making this wedding much larger than my first one. My dress was a creamy lightweight cotton hanging mid-calf with a simple elastic waist—kind of country, plain but pretty.

I was thirty-two years old in 1982 when Dad walked me down the "aisle" of that wheat-colored pasture. Michael and I said our vows on a flatbed truck out in the freshly cut field. The ceremony was unassuming and took very little planning, but it was everything I wanted it to be.

After the nuptials, a popular folk-rock band played music that started reception-goers swaying as the meadow was bathed in the warmth of good graces. Everyone danced, ate submarine sandwiches, and drank punch beneath a tent we pitched to keep the food from melting. It was late afternoon by the time everyone had gone, leaving Michael and me to each other.

We packed the leftover beer into the truck, loaded the canoe, grabbed the best man, and headed to the nearest town where we set out into the lazy Sioux River. Even with a slow-flowing current, we managed to capsize a couple of times. But we were still singing and laughing as we fell into the water, our feet sinking into the muddy bottom.

Floating back to the farm, I couldn't see a single rapid in front of me—in the water's current or anywhere else. Not this time. My future with the handsome swimmer-turned-farmer was something that must be a part of destiny's plan—an indelible stone path, not a side trail or dead end. It was a sure direction in a journey where everything felt right.

But I had been wrong before.

A SAFE PLACE TO PONDER

"Trust in the LORD with all your heart,
and do not lean on your own understanding.
In all your ways acknowledge him,
and he will make straight your paths."

PROVERBS 3:5-6

Dear Father,

Sometimes I feel like I know exactly where I'm going and what I want. Then suddenly, I'm in the middle of something that just doesn't feel right. I think, what have I done? Is it too late to change my mind, to turn around? If only I would ask You first. Please guide me to the place I'm supposed to be. Then I'll never wonder if I've made a mistake, drifted off course, or done something I shouldn't. Help me to stay in Your will each and every day.

In Jesus' name, amen.

CHAPTER THREE

THE SEPTIC TANK

*We must learn to regard people less in the light of what they do
or omit to do, and more in the light of what they suffer.*

DIETRICH BONHOEFFER

THERE WAS A TERM FOR WORST-CASE SCENARIOS. It described
a place—a hospital ward my mentor Dr. Robert Munsick
used to talk about when recalling times before Roe v. Wade
(1973). The Septic Tank was known for its unique female
occupants, women who had illegal abortions and developed an overwhelming infection called sepsis, which is life-
threatening. The term *septic tank* wasn't judgmental, just
accurate. Some reasons why women ended up in the Septic
Tank are so disturbing it's hard to think about them for very
long.

Take coercion, for example. There were parents concerned with how the community would view them if their
sweet, innocent daughter turned up pregnant, so they gave
her an ultimatum: Have an abortion or get out. Or there was

the husband who held a gun to his wife's head, threatening to pull the trigger because he didn't want to share her with a baby. And what about the affair that would be discovered if the evidence wasn't disposed of?

The Septic Tank was filled with victims of procedures gone horribly wrong. Unsterilized instruments, primitive methods, incomplete applications, no follow-up, and floating locations made it easy to have tragic results. A kitchen table, a coat hanger, an enema bag filled with who knows what, and money exchanged often led to infections, bleeding, sepsis, and coma. The women on the wrong side of this deal ended up in the Septic Tank. How many cases could have been avoided? How many women and girls could have been spared?

Illegal abortion was a dirty little secret that cost them dearly—their health, their fertility, and sometimes, their lives.

After my prerequisite classes were completed, I began the arduous task of applying to medical school. The only school I applied to was the University of South Dakota in Vermillion, a tiny town in the extreme southeast corner of the state. My friends in San Francisco thought I was crazy not to stay in California, but I knew I needed a place with few distractions. Of course, I never dreamed the main distraction was now my new husband.

In the application process, there were several interviews with faculty and physicians across the state. One interview is memorable. After I'd driven hours across the plains and sat in his waiting room, one chauvinist MD asked me a question he could be fired for today.

"Why are you even here?" he said, squinting at me unapologetically. "Why aren't you at home having babies? Women don't belong in medical school; they're only going to get married, have kids, and not practice. They only take up space that a guy could use who would make it his life's work."

After he was finished with our relatively brief exchange, the doctor told me I could go, but to make sure to tell my dad hello since they were friends. It's probably the only reason he humored me with an interview in the first place.

In 1982, I was accepted to medical school and began the four grueling years of education as a new bride. Compounding the challenges was the sixty-mile commute from the farm. For the first two years, I lived in a small basement apartment in Vermillion from Sunday evening until the end of classes on Friday afternoon. Then I'd load my cat into my car and drive back to the farm and my husband for the weekend. Thankfully, the last two years of medical school were in Sioux Falls, which was only sixteen miles from home, allowing me to move back into the house. These were the clinical years when students are exposed to many fields of medicine until they decide on a focus.

I knew I was interested in women's health either from the field of family practice or an OB-GYN specialty. During this time my support group was a varied bunch of women in Sioux Falls from all ages and lifestyles—professionals to mothers to students. They had one bond: reproductive rights. This was the South Dakota branch of the National Women's

Political Caucus (NWPC). They were avidly pro-choice and introduced me to the full divisiveness of the topic.

Founded in 1971, NWPC is a multipartisan grassroots organization dedicated to recruiting, training, and supporting women who seek election and appointment to government offices. Interacting with these strong individuals so committed to their principles of women having control over their own bodies, I couldn't help but choose a side. With all of the horror stories I'd heard of grimy back rooms and filthy knives, their cause became more important to me as time went on.

During my last year in medical school, I finalized my field of practice and began looking at residency programs. I had done clinical rotations at the University of Minnesota and the University of Wisconsin to become familiar with their OB-GYN residency programs. But in the fall of 1986 when I attended a conference for Freedom of Choice in Saint Louis, Missouri, held by the American Medical Women's Association—a liberal, pro-choice organization—I became committed to their cause. Their logic seemed so obvious. *Keep women safe.*

Around Christmastime, students prioritized their list for "The Match." The Match is a nationwide computerized program to couple residency hospital/university programs with students finishing medical school. And "Match Day" is a day in March of that final year when everyone learns the results simultaneously.

It's common for residency applicants to shoot high at first, then lower their sights as the rejections come in. Harvard, Johns Hopkins, Stanford, Columbia—any of the top ten Ivy League universities would do for most people. My first choice was Indiana University Medical Center (IU Med Center), though I never thought I could get in. Still, it didn't hurt to try since my brother-in-law had earned a fellowship there, which put family in the area.

Before sending in my match list, I asked Michael what he thought about IU Med or whether I should rank Minnesota first since it would keep me geographically closer to him—about half the distance of Indianapolis.

"It doesn't matter, Patti. Whatever you think," he said.

I took that as it didn't matter to *him*, so I placed IU Med at the top of my list. What he really meant was, *You're going to do what you want to do anyway, so why ask me?* It would be a year or two later, after many lonely months away from him with only a couple of visits, when he would finally tell me the truth: He was hurt that I would think of leaving for Indiana. And he punished me for it my entire residency.

When the lone abortion physician in South Dakota, Dr. Buck Williams, heard about my application, he spoke with Dr. Munsick, the director at IU Med. After an interview, I was accepted.

The first year as a resident (considered to be your internship) was absolute chaos. It was a steeplechase through several categories of medicine, rotations, and study at a delirious pace. Two months were focused on anesthesia, two months on internal medicine, two months on pediatrics, and the rest on obstetrics and gynecology. The final three years of my residency were dedicated solely to OB-GYN. By the middle of my second year, I had already delivered more than two hundred babies. After that, I stopped counting.

In my group of seven residents, there were five women and two men. Unusual. As a rule, the male element dominated, even in this female-centered specialty. But IU Med was different, and we weren't the first class to have more women residents. It was a refreshing equilibrium of equality.

Besides interning at IU Med Center, I also spent much of my time at the Well Women's Clinic (WWC), located in a wing of the Wishard County Hospital and solely dedicated to abortions. It had a private street entrance for discreet access.

Dr. Joe Thompson ran the clinic, and Dr. Munsick was a senior in administration who oversaw its management. He had once been in Joe Thompson's shoes, in charge of the interns, then worked his way up, and was eventually seated in high places.

As we worked in rotation, if a resident chose not to perform abortions, then he or she would handle other women's health care within the clinic. Some of us would do the workup while others, me included, would do the actual procedure.

I didn't plan to become an abortion doctor, just as I hadn't chosen IU Med for their abortion program. The topic wasn't really talked about within the community of students or faculty. The overall medical program simply looked solid. It seemed like a great place to train, and the residents seemed content.

Our WWC patients varied in age, race, social status, and financial circumstances. They were initially evaluated with question and answer paperwork prepared by a couple of nurses at the desk. After that, a physician would do a brief physical before moving forward.

The first abortion I performed was in 1988—one year into my residency—at the WWC, where we received most of our abortion training. The examination room was like any other typical exam room, white-colored everything— walls, counter, the paper covering the exam table—and lots of drawers concealing sleek, shiny instruments cold to the touch.

In the WWC, most of the abortions were uncomplicated first and early second trimester procedures. In addition to performing abortions at the WWC, I also provided them at the university hospital. Those abortions were entirely "medically indicated" due to complications that required terminating the pregnancy. One woman I recall suffered from blood clots in her legs every time she got pregnant. Those clots had the potential to travel to her lungs, which could be lethal. She was also on blood thinners, which put her at additional risk, so the pregnancy was terminated at the hospital for safety precautions.

But there are various other reasons for having a medically indicated abortion, such as genetics. Another patient of mine, a young woman in her first pregnancy, had a structurally abnormal heart. The rule of thumb for her condition is to terminate the pregnancy before eighteen weeks, as it could be risky for her heart to carry the baby to term.

Hopefully, the abortion didn't break her heart a little bit more.

Dr. Thompson, the attending doctor responsible for the WWC, was short and wiry with silver hair and glasses that gave him an endearing father-like quality. He was a good man, and he sympathized with me as Michael and I were living apart. Michael's passion was still with the land. Farm life agreed with him as he continued to enjoy his time in the country. I missed seeing him. I missed our morning runs, our late-night talks, his sweet support. He felt so far away.

At the end of the second year of my residency, Michael recruited a friend to live at Autumn Creek's Farm so he could join me in Indiana. At least that was the idea. We had a few loving months together, but when fall arrived, hunting season grabbed him by the horns, and he was off again.

The months staggered on. Dr. Munsick spent more of his time teaching, writing, and publishing while, along with Dr. Thompson, keeping a watchful eye on me. It would soon become evident that Munsick was grooming me to step into the abortion practice of his friend, Dr. Buck Williams.

As I worked with Dr. Thompson, I heard him tell stories about the old days when abortion was illegal, as well as the added narratives from Dr. Munsick and even my dad. Going through internship back then in a big county hospital, they saw the worst in a ward filled with women in various stages of infection. The Septic Tank was where back-alley abortions met modern-day medicine. It was the last stop for patients who'd given someone money to make their problem go away. Unfortunately, they paid a much higher price than the dollar amount.

After Roe v. Wade passed, it was rare to see complications from illegal abortions, and many residents completed the OB-GYN residency program without learning how to treat serious abortion complications such as uterine perforation or rupture, bleeding, toxicity, and sepsis.

As I followed in the footsteps of my mentors years later, I saw a common characteristic among the patients seeking abortions. They were career women who couldn't take time off and had weekend abortions in questionable settings, underage girls who couldn't tell their folks, non-English-speaking women who were unable to fend for themselves. And then there was the casual customer who believed that having an abortion was no big deal, so she wound up in the wrong place with the wrong "doctor."

Complications varied. A woman could have retained tissue, causing the uterus to try to expel excess tissue by cramping, bleeding, and hemorrhaging, and requiring a dilation and curettage (D&C) procedure. Other cases involved the opposite problem: If a practitioner was too aggressive when scraping a woman's uterine wall, it could cause scarring that could prevent future pregnancies.

And it wasn't just con agents who were to blame. There were licensed general practitioners without specialized training, such as Dr. Kermit Barron Gosnell—a butcher in every sense of the word.[1] He was convicted of murdering three infants who were born alive during attempted abortion procedures as well as involuntary manslaughter for the death of a woman during an abortion. In addition, he was charged with the deaths of seven newborns, allegedly killed by having their spinal cords severed with scissors after being born alive during attempted abortions. In 2013, Gosnell was sentenced to life without parole plus thirty years. He was also convicted of numerous other violations, including

227 misdemeanor counts of breaking the twenty-four-hour informed consent law.

Though you can never guarantee there won't be complications—even in a big, pretty, clean clinic with a trained specialist—it's far too easy in an illegal situation to end up in the ER wishing you had a do-over.

There were too many mistakes. So much suffering. Unconscionable death.

But death can come to those on the other side of the abortion argument as well. For example, Dr. George Richard Tiller, who was a late-term abortionist (twenty-one to twenty-four-week gestation).[2] He was the medical director of the Women's Health Care Services in Wichita, Kansas, one of the handful of abortion clinics nationwide to provide late termination of pregnancy. He was shot in the head by an antiabortion extremist while serving as an usher during a Sunday morning church service in 2009. That was the second attempt on his life.

During my first year of residency in 1987, I wasn't thinking about life, death, and abortion. I was an intern still learning about women's health care. How could I have known what I would face in the years ahead?

She arrived comatose at the ER at Wishard County Hospital, the woman we called the "pink curler lady." She was infected and bleeding—whether or not that was the result of an abortion, we didn't know. And at that point, when you're trying to save someone's life, it doesn't matter. You know someone is really ill when she can't stay conscious and is unable to answer any questions. When you see those patients—septic and losing the battle, possibly dying—you wonder if they'll even survive surgery as you hook them up for a blood transfusion and then roll them into the operating room.

The pink curler lady needed a "full sweep" hysterectomy, which meant removing her uterus, ovaries—everything. Thankfully, she responded to the antibiotics and surgery, and after a week she was able to go home. But not all stories end well.

About the same time, the news reported that a young high school girl was admitted to the ER at a private hospital across town. We heard that she had a fever, was doubled over in pain, and insisted she didn't have any idea why. They began to run a battery of tests to figure out what was causing it. Her condition deteriorated before they could save her. That beautiful girl with her life just beginning passed away without saying a word—not a whisper of what she had done.

As a minor needing parental consent for a legal abortion, she felt she had no other choice but to have the procedure done illegally to keep the pregnancy a secret from her mother and father. She soon became infected and didn't tell anybody. How devastated her parents must have been when the autopsy report showed that she died from complications of an illegal abortion. Millions of questions would never be answered. There would be no information, no closure, no daughter sleeping in her bed that night.

The increasing number of illegal abortion patients was due to laws (enacted from around 1989 to the present day, depending on the state) restricting abortions. These laws limit access to abortion providers, require seventy-two-hour waiting periods (a window of time to reconsider), and require parental notification (a certified registered letter needing a signature before the minor can schedule the appointment).

In 1989, we didn't grasp the physical, psychological, and emotional consequences of abortion. And as a medical and logical thinker, I thought abortion was simply an option. In my view, and with everything I'd observed around me, illegal abortions were doing more damage than legal abortions ever could. In the early 1970s, society and technology were just beginning to change. Ultrasound was in its infancy with muddy, low-definition images. Now we can see everything. Back then, we couldn't. It's safe to say that technology has now finally surpassed our ability to interpret it. How extraordinary, and how alarming.

Back in the eighties, clinics did what they had to do in order to get the consent form signed, thanks largely to loose consent laws. And they didn't offer the abortion patient a thorough explanation of risks as they did for other patients.

If you're suffering from appendicitis and need an appendectomy, your doctor will take you through a laundry list of critical risk factors. It's almost comical how many there can be for common treatments. Yet with abortion, risks and alternatives are rarely mentioned—what can go wrong, possible long-term damage, and what options are available.

We've learned an awful lot since the early '70s, and that should leave very few excuses to keep information from women seeking abortions. I want to believe we'll never need more Septic Tanks. I would much rather see thoughtful, well-considered decisions that take into account the mother's health risk, the extenuating circumstances, and other options besides abortion.

We don't know for certain what the abortion rates are now. The statistics don't show the whole story. New York and California are not required by law to report abortion statistics, so the national figures are not a true indication of current, accurate numbers.

All I know is that we're faced with a moral dilemma that requires the church to respond in a new and compassionate way. The sad fact is that there will always be abortions performed, legal or not, unless we appeal to the *heart*. The true test of our faith is meeting people where they are—physically, mentally, emotionally, spiritually—and persuading them that love will prevail. True faith realizes that anger, resentment, and vengeance won't help women needing love and support during a fearful and often confusing time in their lives.

In order to change the situation, hearts must be changed.

I'll say it again . . . it was never my conscious intention to become an abortion doctor. When I look back at my life, I see that there were a few junctures where I could have been persuaded to go in a different direction. I could have easily chosen a different medical university—for example, the school in Minnesota where the program was smaller, instead of Indiana for a residency. I could have kept my successful private practice instead of selling it to work for Planned Parenthood. If that were the case, would I have become an abortion doctor at all?

I'll never know. But what I have to remember is that God knew what I would do, and He made provision for it.

I love what John Joseph Powell once said. "It is an absolute human certainty that no one can know [her] own beauty or perceive a sense of [her] own worth until it has been reflected back to [her] in the mirror of another loving, caring human being."[3] When I recall the faces of all those women—past patients who came to me for consolation and treatment—and my willingness to bring them peace, I pray that God has forgiven me for the harm I've done.

And though many of those patients did choose an abortion, which the church feels is spiritually and morally wrong, I hope for a mustard seed of faith in a God well able to reconcile the damage inflicted. God is so much bigger than we are—so patient, sympathetic, compassionate, and merciful. And He's aching to give us just one more chance.

You may not see things the way your brother or sister sees them, and they don't understand your position either. But Jesus took all our imperfect works—past, present, and future—and covered them His way. The only way. His life bringing light out of darkness and certain death. Though I might not like what someone else does, I am commanded to love that person, to separate the sin from the sinner.

How I wish we could all, just for a moment, live on the other side of heaven to watch God work. Maybe then we would appreciate God's ever-present forgiveness, accept all of His creatures, and see how equally loved they are by Him. Maybe then we could fully grasp our weaknesses as humans and how far God goes to bring us into His kingdom—together.

A SAFE PLACE TO PONDER

"I believe that I shall see the goodness
of the LORD in the land of the living!"

PSALM 27:13, RSV

Lord,

Forgive me for thinking badly of those who may not know You. Help me not to judge their actions, and lead us all into Your understanding. There must be so much we don't know, so many pieces to the human puzzle that we can't see from here. But You see all things clearly. You have the ultimate perspective, wisdom, and sacrificial affection to resolve all we do and don't do. Place me in a position where I can serve, and give me a supernatural ability to encourage, guide, and love in all situations.

In Jesus' name, amen.

CHAPTER FOUR

IF THEY COULD SEE THROUGH MY EYES

*The voyage of discovery is not in seeking new landscapes
but in having new eyes.*

MARCEL PROUST

AFTER COMPLETING MY RESIDENCY in June 1991, I returned
to South Dakota and took a position as an OB-GYN at a
busy private practice. When I realized the doctor expected
me to buy in to the practice after the first year, I told him
I wasn't interested. So for the next few years, I looked for a
way out.

In stealth, I searched possible locations for my own private practice. A space for lease formerly occupied by Planned
Parenthood—before they began performing abortions in
South Dakota—looked perfect. I moved into that storefront
while still delivering babies at the hospital.

Planned Parenthood took notice, and in 1995 hired me
to work at their new location in Sioux Falls once a week
while continuing my private practice. The principal abortion

doctor in the state, Dr. Buck Williams, was retiring with an exit strategy—to sell his practice to Planned Parenthood. As he phased out, I would come in on a part-time basis to do abortions and eventually replace him in 1996. It seemed like a logical solution for both of us, and I accepted.

Abortion Day—it sounds like a half-off sale or a two-for-one promotion. The truth is, Abortion Day at Planned Parenthood where I worked was just as busy as Black Friday or Cyber Monday. Women waited in line on the day when the procedures were performed. With windows of bullet-proof glass as well as tight security in place, patients outside could enter only with a prescheduled appointment.

With the efficiency of a Swiss-made watch, the assembly line of patients would sign in, pay up front, and then be escorted into a room to fill out paperwork. In another room, a nurse drew blood to confirm the pregnancy, and in yet a different room, a technician performed an ultrasound if needed. One final step brought patients to me where the abortions took place.

Since the clinic did not use IV sedation, the patients were given options of oral pain medications. The technique for an abortion is basically a D&C (dilation and curettage), the same procedure used for a miscarriage or incomplete miscarriage. The uterine walls are scraped, which can be painful. It was important to make the patient as comfortable as we could, but that wasn't always possible.

The prep began with an examination to help us assess

whether or not the patient needed laminaria, a type of seaweed commonly known as kelp that expands with fluid to dilate the cervix. If patients needed this, then a small syringe with lidocaine was used to numb the area. The women would feel a pinch of discomfort as a clamp was used to hold the cervix as a "sound"—a straight metal instrument—probed the opening. After that, the laminaria was threaded into place. The entire prep took about five minutes, and then the patient was sent back to the waiting room for a couple of hours. There she would sit. Wait. Think.

Typically, as the vagina creates fluid and the laminaria expands, the cervix dilates. The further along the pregnancy, the more laminaria is needed. Second trimester abortions (twenty or more weeks) may take more time, even days, requiring several laminaria insertions. South Dakota law prohibited abortion after the first trimester except in a hospital; therefore, our clinic only performed them in the first trimester.

When two or three hours had passed, the patient was brought back into the exam room and placed on the table. Using a speculum and clamp, a string attached to the laminaria allowed for easy removal. At that point, the cervix would be softened and starting to dilate. After a swab to the area using cleaning solution, I did a paracervical block by injecting lidocaine into the cervix at 12 o'clock, 3 o'clock, and 9 o'clock, deadening the nerve receptors.

The number of weeks of the pregnancy determines the diameter of the cervix opening during the abortion. Dilators—small rod-like devices—are used to stretch the cervix opening. I would insert successive dilators until a twelve-millimeter dilator slid in easily. That dilator corresponded to the #12 cannula, a plastic straw that attaches to the suction hose. Finally, the preparation was over, and the abortion began.

The suction machine was on rollers. A clear tube was connected to a glass two-gallon jar on a metal base. It had a pressure gauge that measured the force of the suction, which never exceeded a certain level. A stretchy white sack—a net of gauzy material—caught what was being expelled from the uterus.

Since the uterus cannot be anesthetized like the cervix, the patient can experience a good deal of cramping from the procedure. The suction machine was so noisy that I had to raise my voice to be heard. Counting backwards from ten to zero usually gave me sufficient time to complete the work, while offering the woman gripping the table a light at the end of the tunnel. The whole process didn't take long, surprisingly.

The first pass with the suction cannula ideally gathers all of the tissue—most, if not all. A curette (a spoon-shaped instrument) is used after the suction. If all of the tissue has been collected, there's a gritty feeling to the uterine lining. A slippery or smooth surface indicates that there is still tissue present. Scraping too hard will leave scar tissue. Scrape too softly, and any tissue left behind could cause infection and bleeding.

During the procedure, the content of the uterus is visible as it travels through the clear tube. You can see the gestational sack, the tissue, placenta, clots, and blood. However, with a more advanced pregnancy, a doctor might see actual flesh—identifiable flesh in skin tones—in the gauze sack.

Once the uterine cavity is clean and all the surgical instruments are removed from the patient, the uterus should visibly contract down to its natural size. If it doesn't, then there will be bleeding, which means that tissue was left behind, or worse, the uterus could be perforated.

It boggles my mind to think that someone would perform this delicate procedure without knowing exactly what could happen. It's terrifying.

After the procedure was over the patient was left there to rest, which warded off any lightheadedness or fainting. The suction machine's gauze sack was placed on a tray and taken to the lab for review of its contents. When the patient felt ready, she got dressed and was escorted to the recovery room. She stayed there for a few minutes or longer, depending on when she felt up to leaving the clinic and returning to her "normal" life—taking a memory with her, but that's all.

If all of this sounds clinical and cold, my apologies, but it presents an uncensored account of what happens hundreds of times a day. And what I've described is an abortion during which all goes according to plan. But all abortions come with complications, and the risks increase with each passing week. In addition, larger pieces of tissue can plug the tube, requiring an arsenal of specialized instruments designed for their removal.

After the abortion at the clinic, the gauze sack was rinsed and inventoried for all the pieces to that tiny deconstructed person: two arms, two legs, the head, and the body. The tissue went into a red human waste container with a bio-hazard icon on the side.

On Abortion Day at the clinic, a fairly large waste container would be needed (about the size of a five-gallon bucket), although it was hard to know exactly since it was kept out of sight. At the end of the day, the receptacle was sealed and picked up by a company that transported it to an incineration facility. That facility burned the waste at a required temperature following a prescribed protocol. Over the years, this process has been increasingly regulated.

Fire. It destroys everything it touches. On Earth, anyway. Holy fire, I trust, will be more discerning.

———

The Religious Coalition for Reproductive Choice confirmed what I already knew back then: My practices in medicine—all of them—were absolutely acceptable. And if this alliance of devout religious leaders said that abortion was fine, then it must be true. Fact was, my attempts at deciphering the Bible had failed. I didn't understand it, so I trusted the opinions of established Christians instead.

Since I was an analytical student, intern, doctor, and firm believer in evolution, my decisions were built on solid facts, reason, and maybe a pinch of emotion. Thinking critically and diagnostically as I was accustomed to led me to conclude that legal abortions kept women safe. I considered my services as the principal abortion doctor as being helpful to women, not hurtful.

During this time of working for Planned Parenthood,

I was encouraged to attend pro-choice conferences, including those organized by the National Abortion Federation (NAF). Annual meetings of the NAF were heavily attended by doctors, nurses, clinic employees, and clinic managers. I attended two of them—one in San Francisco and one in New Orleans. The National Organization for Women (NOW) was another very pro-choice group that stole my attention, as well as the National Abortion Rights Action League (NARAL). These outspoken organizations blasting their philosophies all around me continued to influence me and my social network.

At the same time, my knowledge as a practicing abortion doctor continued to expand. The lay term *partial birth abortion* for a midtrimester pregnancy was in the news and everywhere else during the mid-1990s. The medical term for this procedure is *D&X (dilation and extraction)*. Then I heard about a bill banning partial birth abortion brought forth locally by pro-life legislators. My personal thoughts were that the bill wasn't necessary. To my knowledge, there were no partial birth abortions taking place in South Dakota. The only totally elective abortions done outside the hospital were strictly first trimester (by law)—roughly less than fourteen weeks—and Planned Parenthood was the entity doing them.

The only second trimester procedures taking place inside hospitals were performed in situations to save the mother due to diabetes, high blood pressure, cardiac disease, or any life-threatening issues. They were also done if the baby had severe malformations, such as where the brain or heart was not developed and the fetus wouldn't survive outside the womb. In those cases, a doctor had to gain approval from the hospital ethics committee to do the procedure.

Dr. W. Martin Haskell of Ohio, not an OB-GYN but a family practice physician, was the developer of a modification of the D&X procedure. After getting his phone number from NAF, I called him out of the blue and he answered my probing questions. He was doing twenty- to twenty-two-week abortions with a technique that didn't take as long as the old procedure. And the new modification avoided the pitfalls that this late gestation period could bring. And as I had some experience in difficult breech deliveries (both birth and abortion), I was extremely interested in how to make the process less traumatic for all concerned. Of course, his modification would never be considered for use with a viable baby.

As I learned about this new procedure, the thought of one particular patient from my residency days haunted me. A woman came in very preterm with advanced labor and dilation. The baby was footling breech, which meant that one or both of the baby's feet would be delivered first. My superiors decided the baby was previable (meaning the baby wouldn't survive outside the womb). They decided to let the patient deliver vaginally instead of undergoing an unnecessary C-section. The task was assigned to me, being lowest in rank.

Without monitoring the baby's heart, which is never done in an abortion, there's no way of knowing if the fetus is alive. As the tiny body slid out of the mother and into my hands, the disproportionately large head lodged in the birth canal, and the mother's cervix was suddenly in jeopardy because it wasn't completely dilated. The little legs were moving as I cradled the bottom part of the baby.

As I struggled, the attending doctor came in and said to let him have a try. I stood next to him sweating under the lights and the stress as the mother slept. Nothing was happening. A few more minutes passed, and the baby's small limbs went limp as she suffocated. Eventually the baby's head came out. We wrapped up the infant as the mother awoke, giving her the opportunity to hold her baby girl before taking her away.

In my line of work, I see many things—things I can never forget. This was one of them.

But Dr. Haskell's technique decreased the size of the baby's head in order for it to exit the womb without destroying the mother's cervix (not requiring a deep incision in the cervix). The procedure made perfect sense, and our discussion left such an impression on me that I felt the need to fight the ban.

When the bill was slated for debate at the legislative level in 1996, I drove three early-morning hours to the state's capital in Pierre, South Dakota, to testify at the committee meeting. The bill just wasn't necessary for a state where the D&X procedure wasn't being used. Wearing a classic camel hair skirt suit and a feminine blouse with a tie at the neck, I walked in alone. The room was packed, the contention, heated—an expected reaction for such a hot-button topic.

The pro side addressed the counsel first with its argument for banning the D&X procedure. Sitting anxiously as the opposing side made their points, I noticed a woman on the other team wearing the same type of gorgeous camel hair suit as mine. It made me smile. I guess it's a girl thing; apparently, I had chosen the right outfit.

Next, the con side argued against the ban. I had two minutes to convince the committee that the bill would not make a difference in South Dakota. The microphone picked up every inflection of my fervent voice, heard by all nine members of the state's Health and Human Services committee.

In those 120 seconds, I outlined a compelling argument that the D&X procedure would never be approved by the hospital ethics committee, and that the debate was moot. I said there was no need to put such a bill into law as it would never be challenged under the current regulations in the state of South Dakota. And just as I was hitting my stride, my time was up.

I waited at the back of the room for everyone else on the con side to state their arguments. The committee then asked several questions, and the vote was taken.

The bill passed. Why it did, I couldn't comprehend.

In the coming months, I would testify for women's rights at the National Women's Political Caucus in Dallas, Texas. Feeling so strongly about the issue of providing safe abortions, I knew I was exactly where I needed to be, doing just what I needed to do. I had a purpose. A voice. A passion for the safety of women and their ability to access the best health care possible.

Back home, when Dr. Buck Williams finally retired, I decided to sell my own practice and work for Planned Parenthood full time. When the news hit the paper that I was employed there as an abortion provider, the reviews were mixed. While some cheered, others jeered. My dear nurse quit her job, citing with her sincerest regret that she couldn't be affiliated with someone who practiced something that went directly against her deepest moral beliefs.

Back then, I wished people could see things through my eyes. There were so many different scenarios for patients coming to Planned Parenthood—personal reasons each woman had for seeking treatment—though not all I agreed with.

I could understand the forty-five-year-old woman with grown kids out of the house finding herself pregnant and blindsided.

"My husband doesn't know I'm here. I'm pregnant but I can't raise another child."

So she had an abortion. Nobody else knew. She was there by herself. She paid for it. Had it. Left. And it seemed like the appropriate choice to both of us. This story would eventually look charmed compared with what I experienced during my travels in the decades to come. I would see women in third-world countries who had been gang raped by militia, with mutilated genitals—almost bleeding to death—and now pregnant with no one to help them.

Another Planned Parenthood patient, a conflicted young woman, came to see me. At first, I thought she was hesitant to have the abortion because of a moral issue, so I gave her the option of leaving the clinic to rethink her decision. If a woman seemed uncertain, I would give her a chance to reschedule, or not. The clinic frowned upon this practice, since leadership was only concerned about getting the release form signed. But to my astonishment, the young woman didn't leave, even though she was clearly having second thoughts.

"But I won't get my money back," she said, perturbed.

"Yes, you will," I insisted.

"No, I won't!"

She was so afraid she would lose her $400 refund that she went through with the abortion anyway.

As I said, each scenario was different.

I saw this polarizing debate between the pro-choice and pro-life camps as factual science resisting what I saw as uninformed, emotional convictions. How could I make people understand? It was about securing a woman's right to safe treatment. How could they *not* get that?

But eyes are an astonishing piece of apparatus. They blink. They water. They itch. They cry salty tears from a delicate design that is universally beautiful. We take in our world through those minute windows of auburn, azure, emerald, and in return, they bring our entire human experience into focus.

Eyes are small, but sparkling and valuable—all of them uniquely different and utterly precious.

What was *I* not seeing?

A SAFE PLACE TO PONDER

"Open my eyes, that I may behold
wondrous things out of your law."

PSALM 119:18

Dear Lord,

Is it possible to see yet never to have seen? Sometimes I worry that my stubborn perspective could make me miss things that You want me to see. Help me to stay open to what You are revealing, whether I'm comfortable with it or not. Show me the truth. Give me discernment in everything.

In Jesus' name, amen

CHAPTER FIVE

IT'S COMPLICATED

Pure, holy simplicity confounds all the wisdom
of this world and the wisdom of the flesh.

FRANCIS OF ASSISI

STRESS. It can sneak up on you like a silent stranger and buckle you at the knees, or it can march in with noisy successions of pressure and anxiety that exhaust you over time. I had known stress before, but never to the degree I experienced when I worked full time at Planned Parenthood between 1996 and 1997.

In addition to performing abortions, my duties also included dating pregnancies with ultrasound. One afternoon, I examined a young woman of twenty. As she lay on the table, her abdomen extended, I thought to myself, *this is a baby, no doubt about it.* And the ultrasound confirmed it as the data put her at twenty-four and a half weeks—more than six months into the pregnancy.

"You're too far along for South Dakota laws," I said with

a generous helping of compassion, "and you might be too far along for anywhere in the central part of the country."

"Well, I have an appointment scheduled in Kansas in two days, and as long as I'm not twenty-five weeks, I can have my abortion there."

Her tone was flippant for someone of her age and situation. If I had suspected she planned to cross state lines on her quest to terminate the pregnancy, I might have been tempted to tweak the numbers to make her twenty-five weeks. But it was too late. She was out the door with the paperwork, and I never saw her again. It was times like these when my personal views began to muddle and conflict with the establishment.

The same year, the South Dakota legislature passed a parental notification bill for minors, determining that any minor seeking an abortion would first require approval from their parents.[1] The abortion provider by law had to notify the parents prior to the procedure and collect their signature on the parental notification form.

Planned Parenthood was involved in the development of policies and procedures to conform to the new state law. But they made it perfectly clear that as a "mere technician," I would not be included in the planning and implementation of the notification. I was the practitioner, an employee, and that was all. Apparently, I had two hands but no conscience. It wasn't my job to counsel or make policy. I finally knew my place and realized how disconnected I was expected to be.

Gwen was a friend and coworker at the clinic. One night as we were getting ready to leave, she mentioned something without thinking about it. It had to do with a patient I had treated.

"What do you think about that patient?" she said, then quickly backpedaled as her voice trailed off. She obviously regretted asking the question.

"What patient?" I looked at her, confused.

Looking embarrassed and slightly ashamed, she continued, "We were all told not to tell you—we had a minor for the first test case. We didn't realize she was a minor until she was in recovery and seemed a little nervous and worried."

Gwen added that the recovery nurse became troubled when the patient said her sister was home still waiting at the mailbox to intercept the notification letter. Then I realized, like everyone else, that our office at Planned Parenthood had never sent the certified letter to her parents. This child patient had slipped through the regulatory cracks. At that point, the regional director was contacted and told about the incident. His reaction and strategy was less than transparent and decidedly stealth.

"Whatever you do," he instructed the team, "don't tell Dr. Giebink."

I was livid at the betrayal of confidence. Of all people— the one doctor doing abortions in the state, and under his watch—I was the one who should have been told first about the oversight as well as the cover-up. I immediately confronted him on the phone.

"Why wasn't I told about the patient—the *minor*? I'm ultimately responsible according to the law. I could be arrested!"

His response was patronizing. "Don't worry, nothing's going to happen. So we didn't notify the parents. It's over and done."

"But I'm the one who goes to prison. Not you. Not the nurse."

"They would have to prove that you knew she was a minor before the procedure."

Now his true colors were on full display. He didn't care what happened to me. I was there only to provide a service—nothing more. A service better achieved without moral or ethical commentary. I was supposed to keep my mouth closed and my toolbox open.

While I was discovering this cover-up, other tragedies were unfolding in plain sight. In the 1990s and even later, doctors were being shot outside their clinics and on the doorstep of their homes.

In 1993, Dr. David Gunn was killed outside a clinic in Pensacola, Florida,[2] and his replacement was murdered the next year. Also in 1993, Dr. George Tiller was wounded leaving his clinic in Wichita, Kansas, sprayed by bullets injuring both arms, but the shooter failed to take his life. In 2009, however, an antiabortion extremist succeeded one Sunday morning in shooting Tiller as he ushered in church.[3] And in 1998, Dr. Barnett Slepian was killed in his Buffalo, New York, home by a sniper.[4]

I, too, carried the enormous weight of life-threatening danger every time I walked out the door. The majority of women I knew got up in the morning, drank a cup of coffee, and headed to their job expecting to arrive safely. They didn't need physical protection or to give their spouse an extra-long kiss good-bye in case they never made it home. But I wasn't them. In my mind, my job was solely to help women stay safe and healthy, but to others it was brazenly offensive in a charged environment of political polar opposites.

I wore a custom-fitted bulletproof vest measured to my petite specifications by the burly guy at the police supply store, which required a signed form of necessity before it could be ordered. It was high-tech Kevlar body armor by Safari Land. The tag sewn inside reminded me that it was "not designed for rifle fire," but could withstand a 9 mm and a 44 Magnum handgun, meeting or exceeding US ballistic requirements. How reassuring. The double-plated panel directly over my heart posed a perplexing irony. I was a doctor who swore to do no harm, but I could be killed on sight.

Over the vest I wore a Smith & Wesson Ladysmith 357 Magnum—a five-cartridge revolver—cradled snuggly beneath my arm in a cross-body holster. The gun's kick was strong yet controllable. A girl's entitled to some control when forced to pack heat just to open her office door. The protesters marched in front of the clinic every day, and many of them were familiar faces I saw regularly in the community.

When I got home from work, I left my flak jacket in the car or garage before coming inside. The gun . . . I suppose it came in with me. Dealing with the vest and the gun became routine, and after a while I hardly noticed. Since I was married to an avid hunter, there were a lot of guns in our house. I guess I was used to it.

"You can never have too many guns!" Michael insisted.

Now, I didn't just *have* one, I *needed* one.

That year of full-time work at Planned Parenthood was

chaos. It was a comedy of errors, but no one was laughing. The administration hired a high-powered woman to do team-building exercises that seemed useless.

In those twelve months, in addition to the clinic blatantly breaking at least one law, the business manager allegedly embezzled $18,000 because she was delinquent on her mortgage. We were told that an employee stole more than 100 narcotic pills. And strangely, the DEA (Drug Enforcement Agency) and the health inspector didn't show up once. That was peculiar since the DEA has closed clinics for much less. I'd seen health inspectors in my own private clinic and other medical clinics I would work in, but never in the time I was involved with Planned Parenthood. It was odd and yet unquestioned.

At the end of that year, the regional director called a meeting and gave me the opportunity to resign. That's the civil way of letting go of a valued employee. And when I told him that I had done nothing wrong, he had an answer for that too.

"Then here's your termination," he said, as he handed me the document at the ready.

They never said why I was let go, but in South Dakota, employers didn't have to. I had several theories, but nothing concrete.

As abruptly as my job expiration was announced, the pressure bubble I had been living in suddenly burst. Instead of the steady stream of tension, I felt swift relief. I took the envelope, grabbed my stuff, and walked to my car to make an unscheduled phone call.

"Michael," I laughed with a mixture of surprise and liberty, "they fired me!"

I'd worked hard that year, put my license unwittingly in jeopardy, and been under incredible stress. Now it was suddenly over. I'd been released! I had my man and my integrity. It was a beautiful day. We weren't destitute. We had crops in the field and money in the bank. It was actually perfect timing.

It's all going to be okay, I thought with the key in the ignition. *It's all going to be fine.*

"Patti, I'm seeing someone else. I think you should leave."

What just happened? I left for three short weeks to fill in at the Chamberlain Hospital and then came home to this? Michael had asked me to sit down because he had something important to tell me. I didn't want to believe what I was hearing. Michael—my adoring, devoted, understanding husband—had a girlfriend!

Apparently, they'd met just as I was being fired from Planned Parenthood. Apparently, it was a spontaneous lovers' combustion that neither one could ignore, though both were married. Everyone in town had seen them together, so he thought he'd better tell me about her before a mutual friend did. Now all I had left was my integrity. At least I still had that.

Crushed by Michael's infidelity, I left the farm to stay with a family member. Eventually, I rented a cheap apartment in town, leaving everything I held dear: dogs, cat, horse, husband. Living alone again. Feeling abandoned again. My life was traveling in a circle, leading right back to where I had started.

And I was tired.

Throughout the toxic divorce, the other woman stayed at my family's farm! It was a year of complete hell. I couldn't sleep. Couldn't eat. I lost more than 15 percent of my lean runner's body, and you could easily count my ribs. When my mother as well as my lawyer began to worry about my health, I knew things were getting bad. But everything I thought was important in my life was now gone! In retrospect, I can see now that through these trials God was taking me to the end of myself, to the place where He had the most room to work.

I kept telling myself and others, "Once the divorce is final, it'll all get better." But I had said that before, and not so long ago. All I could do was keep going, praying that my strength held out for better days.

Back in Chamberlain, filling in at the hospital as I had done before, I would run along the Missouri River, chasing the water that lapped against its rural bank. Everything looked unusually vivid one day as I jogged past a 1950s-style bungalow. A "For Sale" sign called out a subliminal greeting, *Hey, come take a look!* Many times on previous runs, I had admired that cute little house. I decided to make an offer while following up on a vacant position at the Chamberlain Hospital. And as the gloom parted and the clouds scattered, opportunity turned and smiled. Both property and job were offered to me, and I took them.

The universe was finally drawing a straight line.

It was 1999 when I settled into the lovely town of Chamberlain and noticed a quaint Assemblies of God church that I hadn't visited before. I was making the rounds trying other places of worship, searching for meaning, the reason for being—the usual stuff you eventually end up looking for once you realize nothing is perfect and may never be.

"There's a new pastor at this church on the corner. I think you might like it," a friend told me. So without giving it a lot of thought, I strolled in during a Sunday service, and I was captivated! I had never been so affected by a message before.

The parish was extremely conservative, and being exceptionally liberal and also pro-choice, my heart pounded every time the word *abortion* came up and the room swelled with angry static. Even though it had been over three years since I'd done abortions at Planned Parenthood, it was easier to say nothing in order to avoid ridicule and judgment. My past was safe as long as I kept it to myself.

No one had to know that I was a "Daschle Dem," and that I attended Bill Clinton's second inauguration in 1997. It wasn't necessary for them to be aware of the lobbying I had done on behalf of the liberal OB-GYN Association. Every spring, many of us from each state were invited to the ACOG (American College of Obstetricians and Gynecologists) for their annual legislative conference, bringing a strong presence to Washington, DC. I could only imagine how the quaint parishioners at this friendly little church would receive these liberal connections. My experience had suddenly become a liability. By all accounts, I shouldn't have stayed, but for some unknown reason I couldn't stay away.

Instead, if there was any reason to show up—a service, event, or special gathering—I was there. Within the next few months, I started reading the Bible and actually understood what I was taking in. I had an insatiable hunger to spend time in the Word and read it every day. Soon, I was enjoying a telephone Bible study with a woman—another newbie within the congregation.

Head knowledge about Jesus is what many "Christians" have, but what I was discovering was so much more. For the first time in my life, I was beginning to understand what a personal relationship with Jesus meant. He was becoming real to me—present, loving, listening, speaking.

The journey had probably begun long before. But there are complications of surviving in a world where nothing is perfect. Where your job, marriage, and character are tested, and where your esteemed position and experiences suddenly become a liability. But I was learning. God's unexpected truth was being revealed, a truth I wasn't entirely prepared for.

How wonderful and terrible it is to realize just how precious we are to God, more than anything else—that He would go to such lengths of pain and heartache to bring us back to Him. His emotional connection to us can only truly be reflected in the great affection proved upon the Cross. And it was this truth that was leading me. But as a scientist of medicine, I had been steeped in the theory of evolution. How could I reconcile it within my own growing faith in the sovereign Creator of Heaven and Earth?

My life was now complicated in a new way—an inner way. Do we unknowingly or intentionally sabotage the simplicity that God would have us abide in? All the devices of people, their plans and grand purposes meant to impress, only muddy the living water that would otherwise bathe them in splendid humility. I was learning the truth.

I hoped for a simpler life, a less complicated future. Surely God wouldn't object to that.

A SAFE PLACE TO PONDER

"Behold, I am the LORD,
the God of all flesh.
Is anything too hard for me?"

JEREMIAH 32:27

Dear Jesus,

Why do we make things so difficult for ourselves when Your Word is so simple a child can understand it? Help me to clean out old beliefs that cloud my reason and take me away from Your truth. Let Your Holy Spirit "teach [me] all things" (John 14:26) and reveal how simple Your love really is. And as I begin to embrace the love You have for me, enable me to extend the same healing love to others.

In Your name, amen.

CHAPTER SIX

OVERSEAS INTERLUDE

Cast off all bonds of prejudice and custom, and let the love of Christ,
which is in you, have free course to run out in all conceivable schemes
and methods of labor for the souls of men.

CATHERINE BOOTH

I DIDN'T WANT TO THINK ABOUT THE PAST—my time with
Planned Parenthood, my two failed marriages, the infidelity, the loneliness. I just wanted to rise above it and find an
upper draft that would carry me into a kinder, more promising tomorrow. A second chance—didn't we all deserve that?

I hadn't processed my life incrementally, especially the
previous year. It was easier to file it in the back of my mind
and keep my eyes forward, putting distance between myself
and the changes that were out of my control. Now I was living
alone in a different town, regaining my emotional strength.
That's when I was offered an extraordinary opportunity.

Dr. Vicki was a physician I'd met in South Dakota on the
reservation in Lower Brule at the Indian Health Service. She
and her husband, Pastor Keith, were planning a three-week

mission trip to India, and they asked me to join them. It would be my first excursion to that part of the world, and the experience would be the first of many such journeys.

In India, a third-world country filled with oppression, discrimination, and poverty, the hardship and disease are overwhelming. In a place like that I could really make a difference, albeit a small one.

We took off in early December 2002 and flew to Mumbai. From there, our domestic flight took us to the other side of India where we connected with Dr. P. J. and Mary Titus, leaders of the Church on the Rock (COTR) Theological Seminary and Bible College near Visakhapatnam. Both born and raised in India, they attended seminary in the US but were called back to India where Dr. Titus started a seminary. They also opened a hospital and supported the community in a variety of ways.

After we finally arrived at the church, our weary band checked into the visitor's wing with bare-necessity accommodations and a communal bathroom. Water was at a premium. So was everything else.

The medical camps were usually set up in semiremote areas, either in a school or government building. They were organized and well run, and seminary student translators were provided for us. Our visit was "telegraphed" to each village before we arrived, and by the sheer head count and excitement that greeted us, it was clear our presence was momentous. The numbers swelled. Our medication rations were consumed at a breakneck speed. I felt like a raindrop in a drought with acres of thirsty fields before me.

Much of the time, we relied on improvisation to treat

patients. During an orphan program, the vision test used a motorcycle parked about fifteen feet away. If the child couldn't read the license plate, we would send him or her to the optometrist. The hospitals were so understaffed and undersupplied that even our modest provisions seemed like a gift on Christmas morning. When we closed up shop as the burning sun set, I could sense the gratitude but also the disappointment as the team left town.

With the sound of sitar music, the smell of spices and incense filtering through the hot breeze, and the crush of people wrapped in colorful silk or humble cotton, India is simply sensory overload for any Westerner who has never been there before. Few Americans can picture what it's like to live in a throng of humanity with so few resources divided among a billion souls, and the hierarchy of caste making it even more difficult for those just tenuously surviving. India was a kaleidoscope of varying shapes and shades, and I noticed something peculiar about those around me. Though their cupboards had only enough food for the next meal or two, families were quick to offer to others what they had. It was just what everyone did. Whatever you needed, someone down the street had it. A Band-Aid for a cut. An iron to press your clothes. Whatever it was, they shared it.

For a culture so rich in history, spirituality, flavor, and color, the poverty and homelessness were and remain overwhelming. The destitute sleep everywhere—on street benches, in train stations, on any unclaimed patch of grass or concrete.

To think that God made each one of them in His likeness, witnesses their daily struggles, and loves them at all levels of caste or class, made me realize that our standards of living have very little—no, nothing at all—to do with our value in His eyes. To God we are nothing short of treasure, simply because He loves us.

During the trip, we became friends with the devoted seminary students. As a young man named Romy gave his testimony at one of our clinics, he said something I'd never heard before: "How I came to know Jesus in my heart…" So few words have rarely silenced all the other thoughts in my head. Head knowledge (of Scripture) and heart revelation (loving Jesus) were two completely different things, as I had already glimpsed back at the Assembly of God church.

You can know *about* someone and even spend time with that person, but it doesn't mean he or she is important to you. As it is in any important relationship, to love Jesus is to find a special place for Him in your heart. You care deeply about Him, want to talk to Him, listen to Him, and spend time with Him. You want to please Him.

What an astonishing thing to say about Jesus . . . about God.

From a land so conflicted with beauty and poverty, I always came away with a sense of profound thankfulness for what I had in sparsely populated, aesthetically pretty Chamberlain. But most of all, I became more aware not only of America's abundance of food and possessions, but also our indulgence and enormous waste.

Each time I returned home, I would snuggle into my comfortable bed in the place I loved, taking a deep and grateful breath as I readjusted to the peace, space, and privacy. I was so blessed. So blessed.

I felt like I was living on airplanes. But with every trip abroad, my perspective widened, my love for people grew, and my relationship with God was gradually growing closer. The lens I turned away from myself was now focused on other countries and cultures, enriching my respect for life in all its wondrous diversity. The world was filled with societies that have existed for millennia. There was so much to process and learn. And as God continued to open doors, I couldn't help but walk through them. Our relationship was slowly developing.

My initial trip to India revealed a surprise. My true calling was to touch people living in circumstances they had no control over. It was a feeling I understood. A call in my spirit I had to answer.

And only a few months after returning from India, in 2003 I left for Southeast Asia. I was joining a mission trip organized by a friend's church located in Mitchell, South Dakota. The group decided to go that year, even though the SARS epidemic added another element of risk. Three other doctors were scheduled to participate, but all of them cancelled before our departure date.

All of them but me.

My flesh told me to cancel, too. But much to my surprise, my faith was stronger than my fear. I was learning that God's ways are higher than our ways, and He was transforming me, refitting me for His plan. A physician in America, I enjoyed a position of importance and respect. But just as Jesus lowered Himself to wash the dirt from the feet of His needy mortal disciples, He was showing me the power that comes with taking a lowly, compromised posture.

Cambodia was quite stunning with its sweeping low plains, the lush Mekong Delta, mossy mountains, and turquoise waters of the Gulf of Thailand. If only its four seasons were as agreeable. From what I had heard and can now affirm, they are unofficially listed as follows: Hot (spring) and Very Hot (summer); Wet (fall) and Very Wet (winter).

As our plane touched down in Siem Reap, the incredible temperature outside immediately began to bake the cabin, and perspiration started to trickle down my skin. *At least it wasn't raining.* Since we were close to the Angkor Wat— a massive stone temple where the movie *Tomb Raiders* was filmed—we spent the day there before venturing to the west side of the country.

This trip was also coordinated through a seminary school with English-speaking volunteers. Our team worked its way across Cambodia, stopping where help was most needed, then continuing to travel along the Mekong River toward the capital of Phnom Penh.

I struggled with my medical options in a place so void of social services. Since it wasn't practical to start a patient on medication that they couldn't sustain—like insulin for diabetes—I was left to dole out basic short-term fixes like ibuprofen, vitamins, and some antibiotics. For the most part, we preached good hygiene to the vulnerable and sick.

In many of the locations, I was working from a folding card table with few supplies while facing an array of patient ailments. Our logistics people would line up the villagers and attempt to keep order, but it would eventually devolve into a mass of pushing and shoving. The people hemmed me in so I could hardly move, and the crowd needed constant taming.

Once, the pressure of the unruly throng and unforgivable stress was so unbearable, I took off walking. I found a path that I followed for twenty minutes as I tried to shake off the effects of conditions so dehumanizing I'd only seen them in movies. Not once did I consider the very real chance that I could have stepped on a land mine during that walk, since Cambodia is known for an abundance of land mines—the result of thirty years of war in that country.

We took our lunch break when we couldn't stand the heat anymore. In the hottest part of the day, my mind would shut down, brain cells frying in the still, oven-like atmosphere. It was so difficult to do calculations that it just wasn't safe to treat people, so we would stop to clear our heads.

After two exhausting weeks of travel, we finally finished in the capital city. On the last day of the trip, one of our translators was graduating seminary, and we all celebrated his accomplishment. That's when a student approached me, eyes glassy with tears.

"I want to thank you for caring for my people." That's all he said. That's all he needed to say. He was a strong, proud young man, so the crack in his voice told a deeper story. He knew I was being obedient to God's command to "Feed my sheep" (John 21:17). It's the commission He gave to Peter and to all of us.

During that mission trip, I was the pupil. I learned to be a servant—to do what I was told to do, to follow someone else's lead, and to remain a guest in a foreign land. And as I stepped through a time warp—from ancient civilization to airport automatic doors—a previous thought squeezed me around the heart. We are all God's children, without caste or condition. We all need to be cared for; we all need to be loved and to love.

In March 2004, I traveled to the United Arab Emirates—not Dubai to the west with luxury shopping and a glass skyline—but the desert in the east that borders Oman. Many of our patients crossed that arid landscape seeking care. This time, I needed a work visa in order to treat those searching for help at the Oasis Hospital—a perfect name for such an outpost.

I knew nothing about the Arabian Peninsula, Arabs, or Muslims, and I thought this assignment was probably beyond me—a small-town doctor from South Dakota. But I'd heard about the need for a female OB-GYN at this hospital, and God seemed to be telling me to go. Suddenly, the country was everywhere I looked—on TV, billboards, articles. I knew it was useless to argue with God.

During my time at Oasis Hospital, I also met an American family waiting for their visas to return to Pakistan. They told me about a hospital where they had been working before all foreigners were ordered to leave due to the attack on 9/11. They encouraged me to visit, but they forewarned me of the initial shock I would undergo seeing the level of death in Pakistan.

It seemed that my prior travels were all stepping-stones to even greater challenges ahead.

The following year in 2005, I arrived in Pakistan after a

devastating earthquake had hit the region. I witnessed numb and disoriented villagers standing near heaps of rubble. There was more death hanging in the air than I've ever experienced. Thousands of human lives—in an instant—were gone.

Bach Christian Hospital in Pakistan was another oasis in a hard place, even more desperate than in the desert of the United Arab Emirates. Located about twenty kilometers from Abbottabad (where Osama bin Laden was killed), north of the capital (Islamabad), and south of China, Bach was nestled in the foothills of the Himalayan mountains. Everything there was beautiful—the landscape and the people.

The compound was enormous, with tall, fortified stone walls surrounding it and armed guards dispersed throughout the grounds. At the single massive security gate/checkpoint, soldiers stopped and scanned all cars entering, thoroughly sweeping the exterior and underneath with mirrors before allowing anyone through.

Based on experience, I brought my own sterile gloves for operating and deliveries. Eventually, over several trips, I was able to bring valuable but cast-off medical equipment from local South Dakota hospitals. Everything I could stuff into bursting suitcases came with me—things I could then leave behind for others to use.

Pakistan was the first remote hospital I had ever worked in, and despite so few resources, patient care was amazing. Most of my coworkers were career missionaries from not only the US, but also Germany, Scotland, and other places. The number of patients we treated in a day was punishing. On one morning, I did five C-sections before lunch.

The surgery "suite" took some getting used to. Not only were there fewer options for instruments and suture, but the electricity would cut out without warning. In the daylight, it was bright enough to work due to the windows in the room. But at night, we would be thrust suddenly into darkness, working blind until the generator kicked in again. My next trip, I brought a camping headlight, and many times it was the only light in the OR.

If the deficit of equipment didn't give us enough to deal with, the mortality rate did. Death was all around us, even from simple ailments that in the West are easily treated. But in Pakistan, there were no high-tech intensive care units for preemies. If a child was born two months premature, it was often a death sentence. Still, it was amazing what the pediatrician could do with so little.

Then there were the cultural differences. In the Middle East, a man can have up to three wives simultaneously, but a woman can't consent for her own treatment; only her husband has that right. For example, a patient with preeclampsia needed to be admitted—a dangerous condition if the patient isn't watched closely for signs and treated immediately. But a relative refused the patient hospital admission because it was inconvenient. In the days that followed, I was terrified that my patient would have a seizure at home. A few days later, she was brought in and delivered her baby while there was still time. It was a hair-raising and unnecessary close call.

But other cases ended less fortunately. Like the woman who delivered her baby at home and was then brought to us by family members with what the locals call "fits"—a word they use that can describe symptoms of a seizure or stroke. The baby survived, but the patient was past the point of resuscitation. Sadly, another child would grow up without her mother, not unusual in countries with such limited health care.

The Christian missionaries staffing Bach Hospital are true servants of Christ, dedicated to their faith and medicine, and keenly aware that their strength comes from a divine source. Their example profoundly affected and forever changed me.

And with every visit, I continued to amend my spiritual priorities. How far was God intending to push me out of my comfort zone? Was dirt and despair required to test my past ambivalence about Him? Was I so far away from Him that God was using drastic measures to reveal Himself to me—to get my attention? His revelations were hitting me in waves, fresh and formidable.

I would return to Bach Hospital five more times over the next decade, a few months at a time. After flying thousands of miles to and from, making my way through crowded airports, and taking that long mountain ride from Islamabad to the hospital, the images and experiences are as much a part of me as my own fingerprints.

Fingerprints: They're a stamp of identity. I'm always amazed that it's the smallest things that can have the most detail—minute things, some only visible through a microscope. And I'm now convinced that God's mastery of tiny objects goes well beyond our ability to see them via man-made machinery or even our imagination.

My persistent absence from my home in Chamberlain and the frequent recesses from normal life made me wonder if I had anything to go home to.

Afghanistan was next on God's itinerary. My trips there—in 2011 and again in 2013—were with the Global Health Outreach. A branch of CMDA (Christian Medical and Dental Associations), their teams serve in remote places without health care, providing medical outreach two weeks at a time.

In Kabul, we saw rural people who had lost their homes and were congregating in undeveloped "refugee" camps. Conditions were worse than deplorable. Unlike Pakistan, in Kabul we worked from crude mud huts, unfinished buildings under construction, and vacant UNICEF tents. There was no water or electricity (something the government refused to address hoping it would discourage refugees from staying), and only communal latrines were available. When it rained, the sludge and filth flowed everywhere.

It was a disgusting environment with fine toxic dust that clung to everything and unavoidable human waste in the street. No man, woman, or child could possibly endure such sickening conditions for long and live.

It seemed like a lifetime since I had stood on that conference stage in Minneapolis—the day in 2006 when God commandeered me to profess what I had been attempting to dismiss—that abortion was wrong. The prior years of working with a Catholic OB-GYN who followed God's Word, stayed true to her morals, and stood her ground in the face of disapproval had bit by bit opened my eyes to what God was all about—life. To speak for life. Fight for it. Cry for it.

But with only two small hands and a heart that grew heavier as I gazed at the misery surrounding me, I was simply overwhelmed.

When I couldn't sleep, I would recite Psalm 23 until my eyelids surrendered. Once, around 2:00 a.m., I woke up full of despair but I couldn't remember the words. Out to the hallway I crept with my Bible so I wouldn't disturb my roommates. As I opened God's Word and spoke the Scripture out loud, I burst into tears.

"Lord, what can I possibly do to help? It's all so hopeless."

"Love my people," God said, without hesitation. "Just love my people."

The peace of that truth gave me strength to go on. *I will love them, Lord. That much I can do.*

Moving forward, I poured out my affection on those patients. I touched the shoulders of women who carried enormous water jugs and cradled the needy with a healing touch of compassion. Soon, I realized that I was seeing the same women as they circled back into line for the love and personal attention I was giving away. Because they were second-class citizens in this Muslim culture, the positive interaction was rare, and they craved it. I was speaking the universal touch of genuine friendship, a tongue native to all human beings.

Within this tide of womankind, there was a woman with serious bleeding problems. Sadly, I had already used up any medicines that could have treated her. She reminded me of the woman in the New Testament with the issue of blood.

Choosing my words carefully—we were not allowed to say "Son of God" since Muslims don't believe God has a son—I took hold of the moment.

"A long time ago, my Holy Book tells of a woman who was considered unclean because of her bleeding," I told her. "This woman pushed her way through a crowd to see Jesus. She only wanted to touch the hem of His robe because she had faith to be healed. But Jesus Messiah said, 'Woman, you are free from your infirmity,' and she was healed. You too can pray to Him, and God willing, He can also heal you."

A mix of disbelief, hope, and fear—fear that someone might have heard me—washed over her expression. But the seed was planted. The field was being watered. And I prayed for the harvest to come.

Violence escalated in Afghanistan the next few years, and I was unable to return. But our team received and accepted an invitation for a mission trip to Lebanon in 2014. Again, I packed my bags and headed in the direction of God's leading.

The hotel in Beirut was much nicer and in a safer area than I was used to for the Middle East. There, we were cared for and well fed. I guess that's what made the location of our medical clinic so disheartening. Those we served were located (metaphorically as well as geographically) near a place called "The Dump." At first, I thought it was an adjective, a less-than-kind description for the neighborhood where we would serve. But it was a noun, an actual place where we set up our clinic each day—next to the city landfill.

In the capital city, Beirut's buildings were riddled with mortar holes from artillery fire. Traumatized refugees fleeing Syria and some from Iraq filled our clinics. They were veiled with shock and brokenness, and a familiar account from one patient was repeated by several others.

A family was sitting at dinner—eating, laughing, sharing the events of the day—when they heard a commotion down the street. Yelling and gunfire of an invasion forced them to leave food on the table and run to their car with nothing but what they were wearing. They fled for their lives on a road to Lebanon, finally arriving in Beirut where they now found themselves next to a garbage heap. They made it out, but not all of their neighbors did.

The Dump, where noxious fumes of refuse mingled with the sweet breath of life.

When coming home to the US from such trips, I needed a rebalancing, depressurizing period. I needed time to acclimate to people complaining about everything: the traffic, the weather, their 401k taking a hit. Flying back to South Dakota after a trip, I changed planes in Chicago, boarding a smaller twin engine bound for Sioux Falls. It took a few extra minutes to get everyone to their seats. Then I heard a couple of people behind me griping about the delay.

Inhale . . . exhale . . . don't say anything, Patti. My pulse was pounding.

I thought about a land where my patients were malnourished but were thankful they'd escaped the gunfire. I also thought about how after a couple of weeks, I would be grousing about something too—the early frost or how my favorite purse broke a strap.

As a doctor, it was my job to save life. In these countries I could see, hear, and feel lives reaching out for help. But what of the life that has no voice? What of those we can't physically touch, listen to, speak with? Did they matter? These trips abroad made the answer abundantly clear—they matter as much as you and I. As much as any life on Earth.

As I look back at this extraordinary time of experiencing life and death around the world, that spiritual interlude revealed just how God was preparing me for what was to come.

A SAFE PLACE TO PONDER

"[Love] your neighbor as yourself . . .
And who is my neighbor?"

LUKE 10:27, 29

Dear Lord,

Help me to see people around me as equally loved by You. Open doors of opportunity for me to reach out and help as You gift me. Quicken me to serve others. Bring me closer to the source of divine power—Your Holy Spirit—and continue to protect and enable me to share all that You have given me.

In Jesus' name, amen.

CHAPTER SEVEN

THE PRAYER OF SISTER JOSITA

I waited patiently for the LORD;
he inclined to me and heard my cry.

PSALM 40:1

DURING MY YEARS OF MISSIONARY TRAVEL and a lengthy conversion from pro-choice to pro-life, there was a person who prayed for me repeatedly. She was a prayer warrior I'd never met, but God heard her special prayer for me.

It was the prayer of Sister Josita.

In 1996, Sister Josita Schwab began her work at the Northridge Apartments in Sioux Falls as a Saint Joseph's Catholic housing advocate. After nearly forty-five years of service in various communities, she accepted the appointment of a "Sister Presence" at the low-income housing complex. It was there that Josita discovered her true calling.

Sister Josita would stroll the grounds, making herself known to the people at the apartments, garnering and growing their trust. Many of them were refugees and immigrants with limited English skills. Their fear was easy to understand, since they were so far from home and all that was familiar to them. But it was the children living within those sixty units that Josita immediately connected with. It was their innocence and openness that brought their parents to confide and even rely on this woman with an abundance of grace.

The children flocked to her as she began to show movies and provide coloring books and crayons, puzzles and playground games. After a time, she initiated the first Girl Scout and Boy Scout troops in the building. Most of all, she gave the children a safe place where they could just be kids.

Her undeniable warmth eventually thawed the overly cautious parents, particularly the single mothers. Josita would drive them to appointments, help fill out paperwork, point them toward social resources, and pass along donations. Her ministry of healing and harmony affected so many lives. Along with her summer vacation Bible school and instructive newsletters with information about functions and activities, she held clothing exchanges and relentlessly collected generous donations for this, her passion project.

In the same year that Sister Josita began her work at Northridge, she read in a local Sioux Falls newspaper that a South Dakota physician was performing abortions for Planned Parenthood. That physician, Dr. Patti Giebink, stated that it was not her wish to do abortions full time, and in reading this, Sister Josita was instantly moved to hope that this was an early sign of the doctor's possible defection from doing abortions altogether.

If this Dr. Patti is sitting on the fence, Sister Josita thought, *let's see if God can push her over.*

And so, the nun with the heart of a lion, a woman I had never met, began to diligently pray for me—by name.

For ten years, Sister Josita prayed for me, until she happened to watch the national TV coverage of a vote on a South Dakota abortion issue.

A *New York Times* article had been published regarding the nation's battle over abortion and the vote taking place in South Dakota.[1] It described the Sioux Falls community on both sides of the issue, noting, "The battle over a statewide ballot measure to install one of the country's strictest anti-abortion laws is playing out in television commercials, yard signs, and Sunday sermons."

Now the South Dakota "Vote Yes" bill to ban abortions with few exceptions had national coverage, and it made its way into every corner of the media. And on that evening in 2006 while Sister Josita watched TV, she saw a television spot that more than surprised her. There was a female physician speaking up for the Right to Life movement. When the doctor's name was mentioned, Sister Josita began to cry. God had heard her prayers—all of them, offered year after year. The doctor speaking against abortion was Patti Giebink, the woman she'd spent the last decade on her knees praying for. Obviously, God had pushed me "over the fence," just as Sister Josita had asked Him to do.

And though the South Dakota Abortion Ban (also known as Referendum 6) appeared on the November 2006 ballot and failed, Sister Josita's letter to me did not.

It was now December 2006 (seven months after I had attended the Christian conference in Minneapolis and confessed that I'd done abortions). I had just returned from Pakistan to a mound of mail staring at me as I wearily unpacked. That evening, I collapsed into a cushy chair with an armful of unopened envelopes. As usual, most of it was miscellaneous junk or bills. Breaking each seal with little expectation of what I might find, I came across a letter that abruptly brought my repetitious tearing and tossing to a standstill.

The letter was from a woman I didn't know—Sister Josita Schwab. Suddenly, my eyes filled with tears that threatened to soak the paper trembling in my hand.

Dear Doctor Giebink,
May your Christmas be blessed and the New Year filled
with joy.
   You don't know me. I am a Sister of the
Presentation . . . I want to thank you for your courage
to speak out for life, and the Referred #6 to bring
an end to abortion. When I saw you on television,
I was so proud of you to publicly state that you used to
perform abortions for Planned Parenthood in Sioux
Falls and now you support life instead.
   When I first heard that you were performing
abortions, I began lifting you up in prayer. I do not
believe abortion is right, or a solution to an unwanted
pregnancy. I have prayed for you, by name, that one
day your heart would be touched, and you would
discontinue performing abortions.

My eyes welled up with tears as I took in the words so lovingly written in elegant cursive pen.

I thank God for you, and I continue to pray for you that the coming year will be filled with wonderful surprises from our loving God.

Peace and my prayers,
Sister Josita Schwab

I must have felt the same astonishment, joy, and humility that Sister Josita experienced when she finally saw her prayers answered. And we both praised God!

The strange thing about the TV commercial was that I was supposed to be one of several doctors in South Dakota to speak about the right to life. But because of a production debacle, I stood there alone in the announcement, declaring my position as Sister Josita watched and rejoiced.

Snow, fresh and new, twinkles bright and white and perfect—even in the dead of night. It reminds me of us. Billions of us. Falling, drifting, collecting. At first daybreak, pristine as we enter the world, like snowflakes made of water and stardust in unique patterns. All original. Celebrated. Fragile. A glistening constellation, that's us at our best. Brand-new. Like the beautiful snowflakes falling outside as I drove to meet Sister Josita for the first time.

For ten years, she'd prayed for a stranger! For ten years, she had compassionately pleaded for someone God placed on her heart so purposefully. She'd kept her vigil, and now I would meet this exceptional woman of God. What would she be like? What words could I possibly say to her to show my appreciation?

She was living in Sioux Falls about 140 miles from my home in Chamberlain, a straight shot up Interstate 90. In this rural part of the country, no one thinks twice about driving sixty miles to Costco. I was used to it with only one hardware store, one pathetic dollar store, and one lone grocery store in my own little town. Getting behind the wheel and staying there was like breathing. Besides, the drive gave me time to think—about the gift I was being given—as those frosty flecks of white gently fell.

We agreed to meet at a popular upscale diner known for its enormous freshly baked muffins and variety of homemade pies that complemented their standard breakfast, lunch, and dinner menus.

As I pulled into the parking lot, my adrenaline surged. It was an afternoon in early 2007, and winter's ice dripped in the warming February sunlight. Remnants of snow trimmed the scattered cars as the lunch hour crowd was by now on its way back to the office. We'd decided to schedule an introductory coffee for our first meeting—two strangers with the same Father.

She wore a modified nun's habit: a navy blue skirt and a white blouse with a matching cap that covered the crown of her head. On her chest rested a silver cross that seemed to be a part of her as she leaned in to hug me as I came through the door. I wasn't used to being intimidated, even slightly, though I admit now that some people just leave you in awe.

Sister Josita was one of them.

She was kind and unassuming, wearing eyeglasses and a smile that could disarm a seasoned soldier. When you meet a warrior, you know it—and she definitely is one—from her salt-and-pepper hairline to the soles of her worn black shoes. She had a spiritual strength and presence that more than explained her supernatural ability to stay on her knees until an answer came, no matter how long it took.

Her voice was soft. Not a quiet soft, but a gentle soft. It wasn't weak, just compassionate—sweet but not syrupy. Since we both had no expectations or judgments of each other, we hit it off immediately.

We moved toward a booth, eyeing the bakery case as we walked by. There was only a smattering of people having an afternoon snack. We sat down and were quickly greeted by a server with menus pinned between her elbow and hip. She filled our coffee cups as we ordered muffins.

Breathing deeply, I told her that the address on her letter was that of another clinic in Chamberlain. And though no "wrong address" or "return to sender" was stamped on the envelope, her letter still made its way to me, unhindered. Her eyes gave off a knowing glint that whispered of divine journeys and paths less traveled.

We talked so easily, about my family, her job, and some of her amazing experiences. We discussed the world and the strife that goes with walking in it. Oddly enough, there were no uncomfortable silences between us. It was as if she had known me for a long, long time.

How swiftly the time passed, and suddenly we were taking a final sip from our cups and pecking at the fragment of crumbs left on our plates. I looked at her, thinking what a wonder it was to be in the family of God. I was amazed at how God invisibly moves between His children to bring them together. Now I had a *sister* who felt like a mother and ended up an invaluable friend and defender. We stood up and made our way to the front door. We hugged. Somehow, I knew I would hug her again.

Sister Josita—beautiful and unique as a lacy snowflake—had floated into my life.

As I drove away, an enormous sense of gratitude came over me. A feeling otherworldly. At that moment, I didn't sense any of the world's pressures or problems. Just love—God's love.

Sister Josita still prays for me without solicitation, but especially when I ask for her prayer covering for something particular. She is truly God's saint. Since that time, Sister Josita has retired to Aberdeen to the Presentation Sisters Convent. We write regularly, and I've visited her twice. She turned ninety this year, and other than mobility issues, she's still a vibrant and dynamic warrior. Her initial intervention for me—just a name and a face—moved celestial mountains, making way for my future legacy of life.

May we all stay on our knees until the answer comes, just as Sister Josita did.

A SAFE PLACE TO PONDER

"The prayer of a righteous person
has great power as it is working."

JAMES 5:16

Lord,

*I'm always amazed at how You work through us, covert
until the moment You allow our eyes to see that it was You
doing it all along. Thank you for spiritual connections teaching
us to pray beyond ourselves. Thank you for the Holy Spirit who
enables us to pursue Your will, to endure life's difficult times,
and to intercede for Your saints in prayer. Help us all to pray
for one another, for as long as it takes, keeping us ever mindful
that it's You who brings it to pass.*

In Jesus' name, amen.

CHAPTER EIGHT

JUST LIKE ME

Friendship isn't about who you've known the longest.
It's about who walked into your life, said "I'm here for you" and proved it.
ANONYMOUS

WE WERE AS DIFFERENT AS TWO WOMEN could be, yet as spiritually connected as links in a chain. Simply, she felt like home.

It was the most unlikely of friendships, but putting it plainly, Leslee Unruh was the best thing that ever happened to me, excluding Jesus Christ. Our common threads were loyalty to those we loved, and the betrayal *by* those we loved. Loss was the bonding agent that broke us and put us together. It changed us inside, making us fiercely devoted and not easily frightened. We were immediately comfortable with one another.

Years before we met, a nearly fatal car crash had brought Leslee's dad into the hospital emergency room where my father was on call. Many were convinced Leslee's dad would never walk again. But he did. And he attributed that miracle and his life to my father. Being a surgeon myself, I'd always admired my dad, particularly his creative talent for reconstructing people after horrific accidents—even without all the original pieces. That's a gift.

Leslee made a point of telling me what a hero my father was in her dad's eyes. And it was strange to think that she knew my dad before ever knowing me, that we were already connected. It was one of those times when God keeps a present for you, wrapped and hidden, until just the right moment. Leslee was my gift.

I met Allen and Leslee Unruh in 2006 at the end of the VoteYesForLife campaign, which promoted a bill banning abortions with few exceptions. But their story really begins in 1984 when this power couple launched the Alpha Center ministry[1] on a shoestring budget out of their compassion for women in crisis.

It started when Allen introduced a Tel-Med message in reaction to the local hospital providing an information service for various medical procedures. Choosing from a menu of options, the caller could then hear details regarding a specific procedure. However, the response about abortion merely stated: "Abortion is perfectly safe, safer than childbirth, and legal. It's no different than a penicillin shot."

Frustrated by this misleading statement, Allen decided to counteract with his own recorded message using his office telephone system. He placed an ad in the yellow pages under "Abortion Information," and callers could listen to the message offering women an alternative to abortion. The unexpected volume of calls overwhelmed the system, and it was apparent that what many of the callers needed was a warm-blooded human to personally talk them through their concerns and alternatives.

Realizing he needed help with the growing demand, Allen enlisted his wife to provide a voice of reason and comfort to reach these women. Leslee, a busy mother of five and an avid gardener, took on the challenge with characteristic zeal. She was soon drawn further into this fledgling ministry as it required more and more personal contact. The couple eventually rented a small space and offered additional services including pregnancy tests.

Leslee's affinity for these women was deeply rooted, tied directly to her own pain and the hope of escaping it. She, too, was the victim of abortion, though it now seems inconceivable—as unthinkable as my own past—that this strong, unstoppable Christian had terminated a life and spent years attempting to forget it. Yet her dark past evolved into a beacon, illuminating the way for so many women and their babies-to-be. That's why I've never known her to judge or condemn anyone. The love and empathy inside of her won't allow it.

She has walked a thousand miles in a thousand different shoes and knows the ground step-by-step. Her words of encouragement come easily to her—if not comfortably—when counseling women under the same black cloud of anxiety and uncertainty that once covered her. It is this same compassion that continues to push Leslee to save what life she can.

Allen, on the other hand, was the perfect fun-loving foil to her decorous, meticulous nature. His impromptu tuba performances and impersonations of Elvis, George Washington, and others were enough to easily pull laughter from their grandchildren, or "grand-treasures" as they called them.

Leslee and Allen were filled with energy, genuineness, and an awareness for those needing help. They shared a generous streak—enriching, heartening, selfless—with a tendency to make the people around them better. And just as they complemented each other in their own unique ways, Leslee elevated me simply by accepting and appreciating who I was—flaws and all.

Even today, we are like silk and blue jeans: so different, yet perfect together.

If you've found a tribe, you know the feeling. There's nothing like that special support group of people who speak the same language and discover communal strength, that family of familiar souls who understand each other and know they belong to one another.

The VoteYes campaign headquarters was a hive of activity in October 2006. The first and only time I visited there, Leslee waved to me as I entered the main room filled with a frenetic urgency. It was the week before the election, and there was a final, furious push to get the word out. Since she was the overseer of the organized chaos, Leslee introduced me to everyone. But there was one woman who stood out from the rest.

Her name was Alveda King.

The niece of Dr. Martin Luther King Jr., she was stoic and gracious. We chatted for a bit, and she was kind enough to take a picture with me. It was the day before the TV ads would air announcing that an ex-Planned Parenthood abortionist was now pro-life. Until then, I was still an unknown. And I liked it that way.

Then Leslee maneuvered me into a smaller room to present me to more volunteers and those fighting the good fight.

"I think they'd like to meet you, Patti," she said, so assuredly.

She escorted me into a cluster of twenty to thirty women, most of whom had been through abortions and belonged to the advocacy group, Alive. Wearing their promotional pink T-shirts with a signet blazoned on the front, they were an intimidating bunch. I felt a twinge of insecurity stiffen my spine.

"I want everyone to meet Dr. Giebink," Leslee said so proudly.

A couple of the women I had previously met recognized me and stepped forward slightly. But as my initial gut feeling predicted, several others drifted backwards. They knew about my past. *What is she doing here?* their cross expressions told me. And I began to wonder myself.

I was still getting used to these awkward, uncomfortable introductions. To say I was unprepared for a moral examination would be putting it mildly. In truth, I was slightly overwhelmed, an emotion I was becoming more acquainted with as the weeks went by.

As I listened to their tales of trauma all I could say was, "I'm so sorry . . . I'm just so sorry."

But as our conversations went on, much of the tension subsided as I sensed we all suffered from similar condemnation, disgrace, and remorse. We were sisters of the same blistered sorority, coming to terms with what we had done. While some of the women were angry at abortion doctors, still wanting—needing—to blame someone else, others embraced me (figuratively). And though the invisible rift remained as one faction kept their distance, my presence was healing to others who needed a full-circle moment of closure.

I don't believe Leslee anticipated that some of these women were still resentful of the doctors who performed their abortions. Her mind just didn't think that way. I'm sure she didn't realize that among so many postabortive women, I might have performed some of those abortions. And not everyone in the pro-life movement was as accepting as Leslee.

But as our tribe's common strength grew with each added member, I was only just beginning my own journey to healing. It was time to follow Leslee's lead—my turn to walk a thousand miles.

The annual Alpha Center Christmas party was a way for Allen and Leslee to acknowledge and celebrate the many employees and volunteers who had worked so diligently throughout the year. My unexpected invitation was buried in that pile of mail that greeted me when I returned from Pakistan.

Gazing at its elegant font—no doubt chosen by my stylish

new friend, Leslee—I felt conflicted. Would I be Typhoid Mary again, an unwelcome reminder to women still struggling with the abortion they'd had? Maybe the invite was merely a courtesy from a sweet couple who refused to penalize someone for previous mistakes. How committed was I to this new tribe of mine? Why couldn't I find peace? Maybe it was a spiritual attack from an enemy I was just learning about. I honestly didn't know. But in good faith, I decided to attend. And as the time grew nearer to the date, my anxiety grew as well.

The event was being held at a swanky Sioux Falls country club. It wasn't a jeans and boots kind of affair, and it would take some effort for me to rise to the occasion.

Suddenly, it was the night of the event as I drove the two hours to Sioux Falls wearing a pretty skirt and matching sweater. When I pulled into the parking lot, I sat in my car for a minute wondering if I was really going in. The faint sound of happy holiday music escaped from the entrance, pulling me out of the vehicle with a sentimental tug. I gulped a breath of courage from the cold night air and entered the building.

At the top of the stairs was an embellished table with name tags, printed programs, gift bags, and a woman with an auspicious smile. When I gave her my name, she beamed, and I thought she might have misheard me.

"Dr. Giebink, we're so happy you're here," she said, handing me a program and party favors.

My rigid shoulders relaxed as I thanked her and smiled back.

It was a beautiful event with about 100 guests. Following

an update on Alpha's work and a short prayer, an awards ceremony recognized those deserving extra kudos for their efforts.

I was grateful for Leslee and gave her a Christmas present I'd bought in Pakistan. It was an exquisite gold pashmina—a high-quality cashmere wrap—made from the chin hair of mountain goats. The striking tapestry pattern was hand-woven into the luscious soft fabric and came from my favorite shop in Islamabad. The store had the best pashmina items money could buy, and they were carefully stowed below the counter separately. The store owner brought them out only for people who were looking for the real deal.

Perfect for Leslee, also the real deal.

The lovely evening and all of the unnecessary worry leading up to it made an impression on me. I learned that one's strength isn't in fitting in or looking the part or saying what other people want to hear. It's being your true, authentic self, and relying on those around you to accept and value you, perhaps seeing what you (and only you) bring to the table.

Since then, I've come to terms that my past is set in stone—it is now the Cornerstone that is Christ. No one can take that from me.

Alpha has grown from its humble beginnings into one of the largest professional pro-life services in the United States. What started out as a recorded phone message has transformed into an international organization with a number of employees and volunteers and a 24-7 hotline that is still available with real people to talk to.

Today, the Alpha Center occupies a large building in a busy area of Sioux Falls, South Dakota, providing a full range of services to women and men finding themselves in unexpected pregnancies. In addition to pregnancy tests, it offers limited ultrasounds and programs for life skills in parenting, as well as an "earn while you learn" system to receive points (for attending classes and doctor appointments) that can be redeemed for needed baby items. It also provides a fatherhood program matching fathers-to-be with mentors to guide and help them with their new responsibilities. A support program for women and men experiencing symptoms following an abortion is also available.

Since the VoteYes campaign had climaxed in November 2006, the December festivities offered little shelter or anonymity. If you watched TV in South Dakota, you'd seen my face, heard my name, and chosen a side.

As I became more active and saw firsthand what was going on behind the scenes, I marveled to Leslee: "I don't get it. If the pro-life movement had the same kind of unity as the pro-choice side, we'd have this thing done. There's no harmony on this end. Too many egos. Too much backbiting. Not enough focus. We need to work together for the greater good."

That's when Leslee put me on the board of the second VoteYes effort in 2008. And since I was the treasurer, my name was on every piece mailed out from campaign headquarters. In my determination to rally the troops, I sent every board member a copy of *The Grace of Yielding,* written by Derek Prince.[2] Though a couple of thank-you cards dribbled in, I got the feeling some of the men weren't exactly pleased with me for sharing it. Call me passive aggressive. I don't care.

This second VoteYes campaign was an initiative much like the previous effort, but allowed for "the life and health of the mother, rape, and incest." It also failed to pass by about the same margin as before. In both campaigns, millions of dollars from outside South Dakota helped to turn public opinion.

Unlike 2006, where the headquarters was in a large building in the industrial area, the 2008 campaign headquarters was now in a small building where I had previously performed abortions for Planned Parenthood over ten years before. Planned Parenthood had moved to a new location about a mile west, and this building had been sold to an entity called "Cattle on a Thousand Hills," which belonged to Leslee and Allen Unruh.

Now, all these years later, I had a chance to see it.

My first visit lasted about twenty seconds until I was completely overcome with emotion, a heaviness that took my breath away as I bolted out of the door. Perhaps this was my epiphany, an "aha" moment where my two worlds collided in a physical place. It's where I came face-to-face with not only what I had done, but also with the amount of personal change God had brought about.

As Election Day approached, we were again filming short TV commercials. As I was speaking to the same videographer who had filmed the 2006 VoteYes commercials, we realized the importance of this moment and the irony of the location. We used this rare opportunity to record what ended up being a six-minute video[3] where I walked the viewer through the rooms where Planned Parenthood used to do business—where I used to perform abortions. It was eerie how different it all looked from a new and enlightened perspective.

Those were interesting times as Leslee and I forged our friendship.

She and I were of one mind. We still are. We often send each other cards of support, small gifts, and lots of prayers. We've spent afternoons relaxing at the spa, getting facials and pedicures, chatting all the while. At other times, we've had heart-to-hearts over a bite to eat. When I read Proverbs 27:9, "a sweet friendship refreshes the soul" (MSG), I think of Leslee.

There were occasions when Leslee would ask me to testify before the state legislature. Hunkered down in our hotel room, we would talk about the bill, our position and argument, then sit next to each other in front of the Health and Human Services committee, making our case. It was exhilarating to be on the pro-life journey with her.

Last year, Leslee gave me a Kate Spade notebook—the size and design impossible to ignore—to encourage me to write this book. That's what fellow tribeswomen do. They see your potential and refuse to let you ignore it.

These days, Leslee and I are both so busy that girl time is rare. I miss it. I could have ended up one miserable former abortion doctor, but she took me under her wing, always protected me, and never abandoned me. She was a constant in my ever-changing milieu, and I love her for it.

When you experience adversity with someone and confront the unknown together, it creates a deep and lasting connection that isn't easily broken. My friendship with Leslee has weathered everything thrown at it, and I've learned that personal relationships are as strong (or as weak) as we enable them to be. Like the cords that bind the sails to the mast of a mighty ship, they can be tested only in the fiercest storms. They will either stand the strain or give out in a deluge of trouble.

I laugh when I think of what Martha Stewart once said, only because it sounds like a motto Leslee lives by: "If you've never slept in your own guest room, you have no idea what your guest will experience." And may I just say that Leslee's guest room is a four-star suite. Simply put, she treats people the way she would like to be treated.

May we all take a page from my friend's playbook: Never put yourself above anyone else. Exercise as much empathy as your past has prepared you to give, then extend a little more. And see all human souls as cherished children of God . . . just like you . . . just like me.

A SAFE PLACE TO PONDER

"A friend loves at all times."
PROVERBS 17:17

Heavenly Father,

Thank You for my tribe of sisters who have encouraged me throughout the years. Help me find and nurture others who have few friends and even fewer hopes. Give me everything I need to empathize with their struggles, and help me to be a blessing— a gift to them—as they are to me.

In Jesus' name, amen.

CHAPTER NINE

IT'S A PRAYER MEETING, NOT A PROTEST

In a gentle way, you can shake the world.
Where there is love there is life.

MAHATMA GANDHI

KNOCK-KNOCK-KNOCK . . .

Amy Hofer answered her door, and a woman holding a clipboard started talking quickly.

"Hello, I'm here to ask for your signature to oppose the VoteYesForLife bill on the local ballot . . ."

A 2006 petition was circulating contesting the pro-life public vote in the upcoming general election, but Amy Hofer wasn't so easily won. When this established pro-life advocate was approached by an outspoken liberal on her front step, she refused to sign. That's when I got a call from Amy. She wanted to speak with me—in person. I hoped that a friendly tea in my casual living room setting suited the mood of her visit. But even Amy's slightly sympathetic tone couldn't soothe the news that followed.

"Did you know that someone is going door-to-door telling everyone that you did abortions for Planned Parenthood?"

I knew who this person was—someone close to me—but I didn't know that she was actually advertising my history as an abortionist! It had been years since I'd worked for Planned Parenthood and performed abortions. Suddenly, that someone on the left was using me, the baby Christian growing more conservative by the day, to advance her cause. As I left my old ways behind, which included Planned Parenthood, some people saw it as a form of betrayal.

Nevertheless, I drew closer to the VoteYesForLife campaign and embraced a perspective I believed was God driven.

The next time I saw Amy in my living room, a man named Lou Engle was with her. At the time, I had no idea who he was.

A charismatic Christian leader, Lou held enormous prayer rallies through his movement, The Call, with hundreds of thousands in attendance in multiple countries. As a senior leader of the IHP (International House of Prayer), he was also the president of Lou Engle Ministries, and considered the unofficial prayer leader of the Republican Party. Smaller prayer groups and protests that he organized were often near strategic locations, notably the United States Supreme Court building, chosen to oppose hot-button issues such as abortion.

Thought by some as a "radical theocrat," this spiritual heavyweight was now occupying my tweed couch along with a handful of young people from Bound4Life, a grassroots prayer movement led by Matt Lockett. They were returning to Sioux Falls from a pro-life rally focused on the

VoteYes bill that was held at the state capitol in Pierre, South Dakota. Now they were squeezed into my pint-size house in Chamberlain to meet me and pray for me.

Now that I know Lou, I realize that the meeting was a clinic in apprenticeship. That afternoon he sat quietly in the corner, watching, listening, and allowing the millennials to take control. It was all about the next generation stepping up, praying, leading. He hardly said a word. In an earthly sense, he was bigger than life, but he never stole the glory from God. By his silence, he was encouraging the developing prayer warriors to forge the path ahead. This was, perhaps, a foreshadowing of the long abortion battle to come.

The passion in the room represented youth at its best. So much enthusiasm and inspiration flowed from them, that when they prayed over me and for the forward momentum of the cause, I was deeply touched—by them and by God. They stayed for about an hour before heading to the Sioux Falls airport.

It was a beautiful fall day as we said our good-byes outside. The sun blasted a blinding smile as we looked up at a bald eagle circling overhead. Lou was so enthralled by this omen of sorts—a prophetic sign, he thought—that I almost giggled when this spiritual giant left his suitcase sitting in the street and drove off. His newbie cohorts retrieved the bag and followed Lou in the second car.

Lou was so unfettered in the spirit that he left without his material possessions. But that's Lou.

The VoteYesForLife bill ended up being passed by the state legislature, but lost 55 percent to 45 percent in the general election. In the process I was publicly identified, along with my past, in commercials (seen by dear Sister Josita) that pictured me front and center. That publicity could have jeopardized everything I'd worked so hard for.

And though I was no longer providing abortions, my secret was out in the mainstream, and the uncomfortable facts were judged in the open court of public opinion. When I returned to my church, the members were noticeably tight-lipped. No one would talk about it except for one audible comment, summing up what a lot of people must have been thinking.

"I know we're all sinners," said a parishioner, "but I've never done anything *that* bad." Perhaps she had never read Psalm 130:3 where it's written, "If you, LORD, should keep an account of our sins and treat us accordingly, O LORD, who could stand?" (AMP). The comment was condemning and hurtful, the perfect example of why Paul wrote in Romans 8:1, "Therefore there is now no condemnation at all for those who are in Christ Jesus" (NASB).

But not everyone has been to the foot of the Cross, as my dear friend Leslee reminded me. Not everyone has come to terms with their own sin. And not everyone will. Hypocrisy in the church has been there from the beginning, as Jesus Himself so often pointed out. And the church is where it will first and forever be dealt with.

All I could do was keep my eyes looking up.

The parishioners at the Assemblies of God church weren't the only ones feeling uneasy in my company. An awkward encounter at the house of Matt Lockett and his wife, Kim, in Fort Mill, South Carolina, made me realize how uncomfortable my presence was to some pro-lifers. With six of us gathered together making plans for the weekend, a couple of them who were also in the pro-life movement weren't familiar with my personal history.

Amy Hofer was with me and kept nudging me to tell them. It wasn't my first choice—to divulge such sordid information. I tried to ignore her prodding, to no avail. When I finally blurted out that I had previously been a doctor at Planned Parenthood, several people suddenly became silent. Again, it seemed that the chasm between Christian believer and secular misconduct was too wide to cross.

It was 2007, and we had all come together that weekend to attend The Call Relaunch held at the Morning Star Church, also in Fort Mill. Earlier in the day, I'd asked Matt if he wanted me to speak that night, as I had begun to give my testimony at events and churches.

"No, not tonight," he assured me. *In that case, I'll skip washing my hair*, I thought, *and I'll wear my comfy cowboy boots!*

That evening, the assembly was packed with people as excited to be there as we were. I suppose being present and available made me fair game for the Holy Spirit. I just wish He had given me a heads-up. But I've rarely seen God give us all the details before doing something amazing and usually unexpected.

To my surprise, Matt abruptly introduced me to the zealous audience: "At this time, I'd like to have Dr. Patti Giebink come up and talk to us."

Wait . . . what?

Gingerly, I stood up in front of the 3,000 strong in attendance, mentally fumbling for what to say—not that I always rehearsed everything I said before speaking in public. Less preparation naturally invites an element of the unknown, which can be thrilling and also terrifying. Suddenly, the words came rolling out.

"I'm Patti, and I used to do abortions for Planned Parenthood . . ." There was an audible gasp as a spirit of religiosity swept the sanctuary, ". . . but now, I'm saved and set free by the blood of Jesus."

Like a balloon bursting, that spirit of judgment exploded as everyone stood and cheered. The enemy withdrew through a whirlwind of holy exhilaration. I know that God wants to free everyone, even those quick to convict. And I trust Him for that.

Over the years, I've learned to trust Him for far more. I've learned to trust in the power of the Holy Spirit who enables me to live and move and be (Acts 17:28), to trust in God's grace when words are few and faith is all I have (Luke 12:12), to trust the promise that I can do all things through Christ who strengthens me (Philippians 4:13). It's all about believing, trusting, and receiving the Father, Son, and Holy Spirit.

When I stepped from the podium, a blanket of people enveloped me for prayer and counsel. My terrible, transparent testimony made Revelation 12:11 real. We will overcome Satan "because of the blood of the Lamb and because of the word of their testimony, and they did not love their life even when faced with death" (NASB). And that only comes from a very close relationship with the "founder and perfecter of our faith" (Hebrews 12:2), the One who dwells in our hearts through faith (Ephesians 3:17).

Our intimate Jesus love story brings with it the capacity to transform—others and ourselves—as we share Him with the world.

Over the next few months, I toured with Bound4Life through midwestern states as we convoyed, advancing ever closer to our final event, The Call Nashville 07.07.07 Youth Revival. The open-air venue of Titan Stadium accommodated 70,000 souls. Add to that 2.5 million viewers watching via live broadcast on GodTV.

I tried to wrap my brain around how many people that was. This wasn't my living room anymore. It wasn't a church or an event center. This was an NFL stadium where the press boxes alone seat hundreds. There were ticket agents, spacious grounds, a colossal sound system with speakers, and jumbotron!

As the map and mileage brought us closer to Tennessee, we began a Daniel fast (no meat, no sweets) for twenty-one days, leading up to a true fast (water only) for the last three days. By the time we arrived in Nashville, we were physically drained, but fully armored and spiritually prepared for the following day.

After checking into our hotel, everyone involved— local personalities as well—gathered in a conference room to review the program. The theme of the conference was "Praying for the end of abortion." My sole purpose for being there was to repent on behalf of all doctors who were involved in performing abortions. Amy Hofer and I were seated at a less obtrusive table toward the back of the room—a spot I preferred. At the front, Lou went over our stage schedule. His steady demeanor was reassuring. I gazed around at the spiritual firepower, amazed at all of the well-known people taking part in this Christian movement.

"The Call" was the perfect metaphor for what this was. God had called together this roomful of dedicated servants in order to call others to himself. *It's a call to arms, a call to atone, a call to forgive . . . to move forward.*

"Patti . . . is Patti here?!" Lou said unexpectedly, peering out over us.

My nerves buckled then rebounded as I held up my hand thinking how surreal it was to be included in such company.

"Oh, good . . . good," he said, as he saw me and then continued.

His instructions were clear enough, and I listened closely as he reviewed them. Still, beneath the raiment of my higher education and established position, the uncomfortable inner din of insecurity fought for attention. *Am I really here? Do I belong here? Yes, Patti, you really are, and you do belong here, so pay attention.*

The intimidation lingered into the next morning as the alarm clock kicked Amy and me out of our beds. It was time to get ready—ready for the stadium capacity crowd, the television cameras, the mass of inspiring speakers, not to be outdone by the one and only God who can do absolutely anything, anytime, anywhere. *What was going to happen?*

How far would God go? My heart raced a little faster thinking about it as I put on my makeup.

Makeup? I rarely wore it. But that morning, I pulled out the big guns—mascara, eyeliner, lipstick. I used generous, broad strokes despite a hand surgery incurred weeks before that left me with a bulky plaster cast. Amy knew I never used the stuff, and still she didn't say a thing as she decided that my over-the-top makeover was equal to the over-the-top occasion.

As we approached the stadium in downtown Nashville, the size and scope of the event finally hit me. Tens of thousands of Christians filled the place with an undivided goal—to pray for the end of abortion in our country. Hyperventilating, I swallowed and then took a deep breath. *Okay . . . let's do this thing.*

The stadium green room was quite a distance from the stage and filled with assorted pockets of people eagerly waiting their turn to be called to the substage in readiness to go on. I inhaled deeply once more, which gave me a fleeting sense of calmness before a female stage manager (young enough to be my niece) appeared with a sense of urgency.

"Lou wants Patti on stage *now!*" she called out as if the ground was breaking beneath her.

Her strident pace led me through the mayhem to the substage. As if to test every frayed nerve in me, Lou had already changed his mind, and I was left to idle in agony.

Standing next to me was Cathy Harris, who was heavily involved in pro-life organizations. We had met previously at Matt and Kim Lockett's house—the night I spilled the beans about working for Planned Parenthood. Surrounded by her

own support group—five or six friends and a gentleman I
believe was her pastor—they prayed over her as she was about
to repent for all of the women who'd had an abortion.

On stage, the governor of Kansas, Sam Brownback, was
repenting for all of the politicians who had a hand in legislation making abortion legal. After me, a gentleman by the
name of Will Ford would repent for all the men who ever
paid for an abortion.

Then there was me in all of my gussied-up glory. *Lord,
help me! Help me, help me . . .*

How can someone feel that isolated and alone standing
in the middle of a population thirty times that of her hometown? I felt like a stranger. A wolf among the sheep. I didn't
deserve to be there. Everyone else was a small but special cell
of the same massive living thing. A breathing, thriving organ-
ism that moved in one direction, served with the same hands,
saw through the same eyes. Every single one belonging to the
heavenly collective.

I'm not part of this group, I thought as I watched Cathy
being prayed for. *I don't belong to them. I wish I did. Maybe
I do . . .*

Eddie James played the keyboard behind us, filling the
arena with ethereal melodies. The volume softened when
someone on stage was speaking, then it crescendoed when
they finished and applause ascended like incense.

Waiting alongside Cathy was a powerful encounter.
Together, we were representing all those doctors who stood
over the table, and all the women who had lain on the table.
We could cover hundreds of thousands (listening and watching) who might never get the opportunity to openly repent

for themselves. What strongholds would God demolish when our proclamations were spoken out loud?

At the appointed time, Cathy stepped forward as I stood still behind her, praying silently for her as she began to repent, and repent, *and repent* . . . And as Lou's words from the night before echoed in my head, "You have only two minutes each," a giant imaginary hourglass tipped and drained as the pressure of this moment built inside of me.

Suddenly, as Cathy's words pierced my heart, my body succumbed to the heaviness and disgrace of my soul. I went down—facedown on the stage—sobbing, my glasses spinning away.

I wasn't used to public displays, and I cry about as often as I wear makeup, but there I lay, pressed down by inconsolable grief. The burden of guilt had literally pushed me to the floor. Then I felt the gentle grip of Lou picking me up, and without overture or introduction, he simply placed the warm microphone in my hand. There was nowhere to hide. I wasn't even sure where Cathy was—if she was still on stage with me or not. I guess it didn't matter. I'm sure she understood.

The words stumbled from my mouth. "I'm Doctor Patti . . . ," I sobbed, barely getting the words out. A lone voice floated to me from the pulsing multitude . . . "We love you, Patti!" Then another. And another. Their affection pulled the next sentence from me into the humid southern breeze.

"I used to do abortions for Planned Parenthood, and I repent for all abortion doctors."

And just as these words left my mouth, I felt my atonement and immediate forgiveness. I felt it from the thousands of people before me. From the Father above me. From the angels surrounding me.

Hell was helpless to stop me!

I went on to quote Proverbs 6:16-17, "'There are six things that the LORD hates . . . hands that shed innocent blood.' It's time to end abortion." Then I cried the Bound4Life creed: "Lord, I plead your blood over my sins and the sins of my nation. God, end abortion and send revival to America."

My tears were relentless. I stood there, humbled to the core, unable to move. Cindy Jacobs, an author, speaker, and prayer warrior, wrapped her arms around me and spoke directly into the microphone: "For all the mothers and grandmothers who will never hold their children and grand-children, we forgive you."

Lou squeezed us both, and my heart broke a little more as I cried harder thinking of all the babies whose lungs would never breathe in sweet air, shed happy tears of joy, feel the love of a human embrace—because of *me*. I couldn't bring them back to life, but I could speak out for the future lives that were predestined to come.

And the makeup ran! Black non-waterproof mascara down to my chin—all captured on the jumbotron!

Two minutes: That's how long it took for God to completely restore me. The shameful scars of what I had done were now valuable currency on redemption's exchange. My soul soared . . . like Lou's eagle. I could finally fly free! God knew exactly what I needed—what it would take to deliver me. I just can't believe GodTV got it all on tape with millions of viewers watching![1] *Lord, why?* But we know why.

As I looked out at those faces rinsed in the Tennessee

summer sun, I thought of heaven. In heaven, all of us become one (in the Spirit), reconciled under One (Christ), and forgiven by One (the Father). We're no longer alone. Every person is equally loved and bathed in the light of God. I could feel something happening.

My presence there was needed, even necessary, for the fight to be won. In a profound and healing way, I *did* belong there. Joined by the Spirit, without anger or resentment, with transparency and understanding, we will bring about change. By raising our voices.

Not in protest, but in loving prayer.

A SAFE PLACE TO PONDER

"Hatred stirs up strife, but love covers all offenses."

PROVERBS 10:12

Father,
  You're up to something, and it's good! It's always good. And while my flesh tells me I can't do it, my faith knows that in Christ, I can. No matter how scary or overwhelming it looks, You're there waiting for me in the midst of it. You go ahead of me and behind me. You hem me in on all sides. Continue to lead me where kings tread; use my voice to repent for my generation because I know that where love is, there is life.
  In Jesus' name, amen.

CHAPTER TEN

FAN MAIL TO A FEMINAZI

Rash language cuts and maims,
but there is healing in the words of the wise.
PROVERBS 12:18 (MSG)

I LAUGHED IN DISBELIEF THE FIRST TIME I read it. But it wasn't as funny the second or third time. Particularly when I was carrying a loaded gun into work and starting to feel normal about it. Still, the word *feminazi* had an inventive satirical quality that set the letter apart from the rest of the hate mail I was getting at Planned Parenthood from 1995 to 1997. It communicated the usual animosity that I was becoming accustomed to, but at least it was original.

Most of the threatening letters and suspicious packages that came through the US Postal Service were vetted. For example, envelopes were set aside if they had certain distinct features such as a typed recipient but no return address, or better yet, words, letters, and numbers clipped from magazines and glued to the paper, like the stuff you see on cop shows. In those cases, the post office would notify the FBI directly, and they would send an agent to pick up that mail. Even so, some of the letters made their way to the clinic. The letter calling me a feminazi was one of them.

It was strange to find myself in such a close relationship with the local police force and Federal Bureau of Investigation, which would follow up on any credible threats. But it was happening all over the country. Planned Parenthood facilities and their employees were under siege, so it felt as though I was serving on the front line. *Serving.* That was exactly what I believed I was doing. Fighting for women and their right to safe health care. And as I understood the law, that wasn't a crime.

———

Pages of praise and disapproval continued to find their way to me. They were handwritten, typed, and emailed. Some of the senders I knew—patients and colleagues. Others I had never met, but over time their zeal crept into my mailbox as my life aligned with one side of the abortion debate or the other.

Words have power; a vibration when spoken (or read) that can soothe or destroy. God spoke and there was light. He created everything through the Word. We say words all day long, but few really catch our attention except the ones that scrape and bite. Over the years, I've heard all kinds of words within comments and letters sent to me. The following are just a few that cover the gamut between the pro-choice and pro-life camps.

From a businesswoman and friend:

April 12, 1995

Dear Patti:
Since I haven't seen you lately and it will be awhile before
I see you again, I just wanted to send you a letter of
support and encouragement. I noticed the article in the
Argus today about your assistance to Planned Parenthood.
I know there are many people that appreciate your
convictions. I can also understand many reasons why it
is difficult to discuss the topic with the media. However,
this is such an important "women's right to privacy" issue.

Best regards,
Kensey

This was a kind reinforcement that I received after the local
newspaper published an article about my new job at Planned
Parenthood. I appreciated it, as I did this one from an anonymous source:

Dear Dr. Giebink,
I just wanted to let you know that you do have support
from people for the service you are providing at Planned
Parenthood. People like Paul Dorr [of Iowa] have
no business telling any female what she should or
shouldn't do.
I was against abortion until I was faced with being
pregnant at nineteen years old, unmarried, a victim
of date rape, working two part-time jobs to put myself

through college, had no money, very little support from
anyone, and terrified of my parents' reaction to their
almost "saintly" daughter getting pregnant! I felt I had
no other choice.

I don't know if I made the right decision, but at
least I had a choice! You are providing a service to others
in my position that could otherwise take more drastic
measures—dangerous ones.

I sincerely hope you will continue the practice
you have privately, as well as the services you provide
elsewhere. I pray that the Right to Life groups who tend
to get out of control will not try to harm you, your staff,
or any of your patients.

Signed,
A Concerned Sioux Falls Resident

At first, it seemed that the community consensus was of one
mind—that what I was doing was right and good. Then I'd
get a letter that would begin that way, but then turn in a
direction my heart wasn't ready for. Like this one:

Dear Dr. Giebink,
I'm writing to thank you for the care you gave me
prenatally and postpartum. I felt you were caring and
respectful of me. I appreciate you allowing me to have
input in my care.

I must, however, cease our patient/physician
relationship due to the decision you have made to do
abortions. I have heard that this will be a part of your
practice. If I have wrong information, please let me know.

*I cannot support the ending of life, especially after I
tried so hard to have children. After years of infertility,
I would have done anything to have a baby. The
waiting list for adoption is extremely long, and I was
not even close to receiving a baby. Fortunately, I was
able to conceive not just once, but twice. Those who are
not as lucky as I am may wait ten years until they can
hold a baby.*

    *This is not a letter of intent to reprimand, but to see
another aspect of the issue.*

Sincerely,
Miranda

Okay, that one stung. This was a lovely patient of mine, and I
took pride in caring for her through and after her pregnancy.
Now this. But as God was busy peeling back the layers of
this onion, my media platform reached further. And with
the incredible people I was meeting and the ongoing spiritual experiences unfolding day by day, the tone of the letters
began to reflect the changes happening in me:

Dear Patti Giebink,
*I am sending this letter to express in a special way my
thankfulness to God and to you for your total change
of heart in regard to the culture of life. Perhaps you do
not have the same name recognition as a Dr. Bernard
Nathanson, but it goes without saying it has the same
connotation to us who know you and your former
position. Surely the good Lord has totally forgiven you
and welcomed you back with His arms wide open.*

I truly think it's marvelous of you to put your name
in such a conspicuous place, before all and God to
see as treasure of this "love life organization." For you
especially, it had to take a great amount of fortitude
to say yes to accept this visibility.

Warmly,
Paul W. Scholten

That particular letter meant a great deal to me, since this was the man who coined that imaginative word *feminazi* found in that earlier letter he sent to me. I only wish I had kept a copy as his wife, Shirley, assures me that though Paul has gone to be with the Lord, he would have gotten a kick out of his initial message being shared in this book.

How many people can a single person touch? It makes me think of *It's a Wonderful Life* where Clarence the angel allows Jimmy Stewart to see the world around him as if he had never been born. Only I was seeing how my seemingly small, reasonable actions were adversely affecting those around me. The following letter made that abundantly clear:

Dear Dr. Giebink,
My name is Renae Green. I was one of your patients
eighteen years ago. In 1995, I was pregnant with my fifth
child. We were very excited and thrilled another baby
was going to join our family. On Mother's Day, while
I was in Omaha for my sister's baby shower, I began
miscarrying and was very distraught. I had never had
any problems with previous pregnancies, so I was shocked
that something like this was happening to me.

FAN MAIL TO A FEMINAZI

My other children were just thirteen, four, three, and two years old. They were excited about the prospect of having a baby, and on that Mother's Day as they were giving me gifts, I remember trying to figure out a way to tell them this baby was in heaven. I cried bitter, angry tears. I felt like I was losing something so precious, and no one else understood.

When we arrived back in Sioux Falls, we came to see you. An ultrasound was done to correctly diagnose the miscarriage. I had an inkling of hope until I saw the black screen. That tiny beating heart was nowhere to be found. At three months gestation, I had thought I was in the clear, but God had different plans.

I began to bleed heavily at home, and again we came to see you when the hemorrhaging was so intense that I was feeling weak. You did a D&C. I remember the prep room. I was still feeling the hot burning tears as they ran down my cheeks. I was still questioning God . . . I asked that question over and over again, "Why?"

The nurses were all very sweet and caring. But what I remember most was you. I remember the compassion and love you showed me that day. I remember that look of concern and care, and the calming words you had for me. I especially remember how you held my hand as I drifted off to sleep before the procedure began. I want to thank you for bringing a little peace to my soul on that horrible day.

Then the following year, I again was pregnant. On April 19, 1996, you delivered to our family one of our most precious gifts we had ever received. You remembered

*the miscarriage just a year before, so when you saw my
tears of relief and joy that day, you understood.*

*It was shortly after my daughter's birth that
I had learned that you had performed abortions.
I was absolutely devastated. I couldn't wrap my head
around how someone who cared so much and was so
compassionate during my miscarriage could turn around
and terminate other little ones on purpose. I was very
bitter. I kept seeing that look on your face as you held my
hand and comforted me . . . it just didn't make sense.*

*Then I found out that you had changed. Your heart
had changed, and you realized that the services you were
providing these women were wrong. I was overjoyed
when I saw your commercial on TV. I was extremely
proud of you in being able to face the public and admit
to everyone that what you were doing was not right. It
had to be so hard.*

*Right then, my bitterness towards you was gone. I
felt very proud to tell the story of this wonderful doctor
who stood up for a cause that is so dear to my heart. You
speak for those who have no voice. You give these babies a
chance to become great and vibrant leaders of our society.*

*Patti, I want to thank you for everything. I want to
thank you for being there when I really needed you. I
want to thank you for the gift of my sweet daughter. But
most of all, I want to thank you for your support of all
life. How precious each little life is, and who knows
what each one may one day accomplish.*

May God's blessings for you be abundant!

Love, Renae

It's difficult to put into words exactly what this letter means to me, and how it proves that every act of kindness or carelessness affects the people connected to us. Our views, decisions, and reevaluations in life can have profound and lasting meaning to others who may be watching, and to those who might be praying.

Dr. Ben Anderson was a colleague practicing near Sioux Falls. He is a spiritual heavyweight, and one of the kindest men I've known. His transparency and willingness to ask the tough questions in love was a truly inspiring work of God. The following correspondence between us is something I cherish:

May 31, 1995

Dear Pat,
It was recently reported to me that you have begun
providing abortions for Planned Parenthood in Sioux
Falls. I am very interested to know if that is true. If it is,
I would appreciate to know the reasons and motivations
that led you to that decision. I look forward to your reply.
Sincerely,
Ben Anderson, M.D.

Reading his letter now, I'm impressed by the level of calm respect this Christian man showed me—a nonbeliever and fellow physician practicing methods he staunchly opposed. This was my response on June 19, 1995.

Dear Ben,

Thank you for your letter of May 31, 1995. I have been pondering a reply since that time.

I began doing abortions one day a week for Planned Parenthood in Sioux Falls last February. There was an article in the Sioux Falls Argus Leader in mid-April to that effect. Without knowing how you feel about this issue, let me answer your question.

The reason I decided to start doing abortions has to do with my strong feeling that abortion must be available, safe, and legal. Prior to Roe v. Wade in 1973, the abundance of illegal and unsafe abortions is well documented. In the last few years, as abortion has become less available, there has been a rise again in back-alley abortions.

Regardless of one's feeling toward abortion, no one can ignore the dangers of abortion in the wrong hands.

The emphasis needs to be placed on preventing unwanted pregnancy. Unfortunately, the same forums against safe, legal abortions are also opposed to sex education and birth control. I think all of us would rather see a decline in the need for abortion through education and abstinence or contraception.

I realize that you work in an area of the country that is deeply religious. I have enclosed a brochure from the RCAR, the Religious Coalition for Abortion Rights. The people we see in the clinic are from all walks of life and religious backgrounds. Frequently, when I ask a woman how long she has been pro-choice, her answer is often "five or ten minutes." Women do not choose

*abortion callously or frivolously. This is a decision that
they reach through much forethought and consideration
of the alternatives.*

*I knew when I made this decision it might not
be popular with some people. The response has been
overwhelmingly supportive. The people of Sioux Falls
may not be outwardly and publicly vocal, however,
privately many people have given me encouragement.
I have lost a few patients, but I have certainly gained
an equal number.*

*I am grateful that you sent a letter giving me an
opportunity to explain my position. I hope that this does
not interfere with our professional relationship. I have
enjoyed working with you, and I hope we can continue.*

*If you have any further questions or need any further
information, please do not hesitate to call.*

*Respectfully,
Patricia K. Giebink, M.D.*

Our professional relationship remained unscathed while he
retained his solid view on the matter, which was definitively
pro-life. I sent my follow-up letter several years later.

March 7, 2012

*Dear Ben,
I ran across a letter you wrote to me May of 1995 when
I was cleaning out boxes of papers in my basement. I
also had a copy of my response in the file. Now what I
said seems laughable to me. I'm sending you this issue*

*of Pentecostal Evangel because I am the cover story—
about what God has done in my life. It's a good article
and I hope it is a benefit to you.*

*Since 1999, I've lived in Chamberlain, South
Dakota. Until about three and a half years ago I was
working here at the hospital. Now I do locum tenens
[substitute practice] and missions. Your 1995 letter was
concerning my starting to work at Planned Parenthood
and my reasons for it. It's amazing that I kept it.
Perhaps so I could send you the magazine. Perhaps as
a reminder to me that God does indeed work miracles!*

*Blessings in Christ,
Patti Giebink*

God's miracles abound in the most unlikely ways. But He *is*
the God of the impossible! And as you read Dr. Anderson's
response, you'll agree that there is nothing God cannot do.

May 2012

*Dear Patti,
It's been a couple of months now since I received your
unexpected correspondence. I apologize for my delay in
answering.*

*Your letter was as rich a blessing as I have had
in a very long time. I actually wanted to reflect on
it for a while before responding. My initial emotion
was to marvel at the way in which God sovereignly
and graciously weaves the tapestry of our lives for
His glory and our good.*

After 1995, I remember hearing that you had moved to Chamberlain, but not knowing why. Seventeen years tends to cloud my memory a bit, but I do remember writing you and you responding. Time, age, and God's grace have hopefully mellowed and matured me some, so though my convictions have not changed, I only hope that my letter was a balance of truth and grace. If it is of any value, you are welcome to use it as you wish.

More importantly, I am still rejoicing to hear how the Lord saved you and is using you in His kingdom. The article does not detail how you came to faith, but I would love to hear. It is good we can share the knowledge that the blood of Christ covers all our sins, yours and mine. It is a joy to see your involvement in overseas missions and pro-life advocacy at home. Both can seem to be uphill challenges at times. My wife and I have had the privilege to be involved with a Sioux Falls–based medical mission organization, The Luke Society.

Patti, I could tell from your letter, the article, and the YouTube video that your past experiences have left some painful scars. I cannot help but think of Ephesians 2:

> *And you were dead in the trespasses and sins in which you once walked, following the course of this world, following the prince of the power of the air, the spirit that is now at work in the sons of disobedience—among whom we all once lived in the passions of our flesh, carrying out the desires*

of the body and the mind, and were by nature
children of wrath, like the rest of mankind.
But God . . .

EPHESIANS 2:1-4

Among whom we all once lived—that's you, me, and
everybody. But God . . . made us alive together with
Christ, by grace alone. Sola Deo Gloria. I am very
thankful that you took the time to write me. I would
enjoy the opportunity to connect further.
May God richly bless you.

Your brother in Christ,
Ben Anderson

I think of the letters that were written by the apostle Paul in prison. The ones that were carried by foot, horseback, and boat to distant Christian outposts during turbulent times; they are still as powerful to read today as they were before.

May we choose our words cautiously and may our gentleness be evident to all. May these words not be declarations written with pens of poison. I pray for words that lift, restore, heal, and bring others to the hope of God.

Yes, words can be powerful envoys of beauty or of ugliness. And whether I'm viewed as a saint to some or a feminazi to others, I am now choosing to use my own words for good. I want this book to be filled with reassurance and inspiration to women who need a friend, a like-spirit, and a kind word.

A SAFE PLACE TO PONDER

"Blessed are the merciful,
for they shall receive mercy."

MATTHEW 5:7

Jesus,

I realize my words have the power to heal or harm. And depending on how I'm feeling, they can do either one. Keep my heart and words stayed on You, so that the people around me will be blessed, encouraged, and motivated to do the same for others.

In Jesus' name, amen.

CHAPTER ELEVEN

A UNIQUE HUMAN BEING

Each human being is bred with a unique set of potentials that yearn to be fulfilled as surely as the acorn yearns to become the oak within it.

ARISTOTLE

WHAT MAKES US EACH A UNIQUE PERSON? Our hair, our eyes, the color of our skin? Our opinion or political position? What makes us distinct personalities? Is it living on a particular continent or in one hemisphere or the other? Is it due to our citizenship in a developed country with constitutional rights and an established democracy, or our residence in the third world with a tyrannical leader or rogue militia?

With billions of souls inhabiting the planet, how many truly unique people are there? Is it our vanity that says we're unique? Is nature simply unable to duplicate something? Or does Father God's enduring commitment to individuality keep Him from creating identical articles—living or lifeless?

What makes a human being unique?

South Dakota created landmark pro-life legislation to answer that question. In 2005, the state legislature passed the "informed consent" law that established "beyond dispute that the unborn child is a whole, separate, unique, living human being from fertilization to full gestation." And that abortion posed "profound risk of physical and psychological harm to the mother, including suicidal ideation and suicide."

Immediately, Planned Parenthood filed an injunction to prevent enforcement of this law. After seven plus years and several trips to the US Eighth Circuit Court of Appeals in St. Louis, Missouri, I've witnessed the approval of all sections of the law, most notably the disclosure that abortion ends the life of a "whole, separate, unique, living human being."

For those who are unfamiliar with how the appeals system works, allow me to fill in some of the blanks. The US has twelve appellate circuit courts including eleven districts of states and Washington, D.C. The Eighth Circuit Court hears cases from the states of North Dakota, South Dakota, Nebraska, Minnesota, Iowa, Missouri, and Arkansas. The court has a total of eleven judges, but usually a panel of three hears appeal cases. A full panel of eleven is called "en banc" and is somewhat rare.

But why is informed consent so important?

For years—since Roe v. Wade was made law by the Supreme Court in 1973—"informed consent" was vaguely described at best. Abortion clinics told pregnant women that the growing baby inside them was "just tissue" and often used the phrase "contents of the uterus" instead of the word *fetus* in order to expedite the signing of the consent form.

Now, since 2009 in South Dakota, written consent for

an abortion must include the sentence "abortion terminates the life of a whole, separate, unique, living human being . . . Established beyond dispute that the unborn child is a whole, separate, unique, living human being from fertilization to full gestation."

There is no longer any confusion about the goal and end result of an abortion. The law is intended to protect women from misleading language that diminished the act of abortion.[1] It was based on a large body of scientific evidence and hours of testimony by experts in science and medicine. This culminated more than thirty years of trying to confirm the rights of the child in utero.

One argument used against this informed consent bill claimed that it interfered with a doctor's First Amendment right of free speech. In any other informed consent for a medical procedure, nearly every possible risk and complication is mentioned, including those that are rare or even theoretical.

For instance, prior to my common nasal sinus surgery, the doctor provided all possible risks as part of the verbal informed consent, including "the possibility of dripping spinal fluid from my nose" following surgery, even though he had never seen that happen. I thought that because I was a physician, my doctor wanted to cover all the bases. But why didn't the doctors and others explain the risks of abortion in such graphic detail to the women considering the procedure?

It's well known in my field of obstetrics that OB doctors have two patients to take care of: mom and baby. The goal at the end of nine months is a happy, healthy mother and a strong, vibrant child. And everything we do is based on that goal. Two humans—both viable, important, and independent of each other.

The second part of the South Dakota statute is based on the relationship a woman has with her unborn child. Abortion advocates contended that it's a woman's right to have an abortion based on the 1973 Supreme Court Roe v. Wade decision. However, the state statute revealed that abortion actually terminates a woman's right—the basic inherent right a mother has for a relationship with her child.

Look at it this way: This same relationship has long been recognized in the process of adoption. In fact, great steps are taken so the biological parents understand they are giving up their parental rights. They are provided a window of time to change their minds, revoke their decision, and keep their intrinsic right to a relationship with their child.

The Eighth Circuit Court affirmed the disclosure of this "parental right of relationship" on the informed consent document for abortion. Therefore, a woman understands that she is giving up that right (bond) with her unborn child prior to undergoing a permanent, irreversible procedure. The mother contemplating an abortion is not exercising a right, she is contemplating waiving or surrendering the most important intrinsic natural right she possesses other than her own right to life.

The final section of the South Dakota 2005 informed consent law concerns the disclosure that undergoing an abortion may result in "profound risk of physical and psychological harm to the mother, including suicidal ideation and suicide." This is something Planned Parenthood adamantly disagrees with as stated on its own disclosure form:

*Planned Parenthood believes this statement is wrong
and/or misleading. Planned Parenthood believes that
the reliable medical evidence does not demonstrate that
abortion actually causes suicide or thought of suicide.*

Abortion advocates propose that only women with mental
and/or psychological problems prior to an abortion will suffer psychological effects after an abortion. Even the American
Psychiatric Association (APA) approves and points to studies that agree with this claim, but it refuses to acknowledge
a large body of scientific evidence to the contrary. Another
substantial group of medical professionals, the American
College of Obstetricians and Gynecologists (ACOG) also
refuses to accept studies that don't concur with their beliefs,
and excludes opposing studies no matter how thorough and
well performed they are.

Another growing body of medical professionals, the
American Association of Pro-Life Obstetricians and
Gynecologists (AAPLOG) has amassed scientific studies
that present different views and conclusions. For years,
this association has been trying to bring balance to the
scientific literature, yet has been denied from publishing in certain elite medical journals. Its website, however
(https://aaplog.org), is a user-friendly library of important
information.

Finally, in December of 2012, an en banc panel (all eleven
judges) ruled to include the suicide disclosure on all informed
consents for an abortion in South Dakota—stating that abortion increases a woman's risk of depression and thoughts of
suicide, with the potential to harm herself.

One thing we discovered following both VoteYes campaigns was that many women realized their emotional problems arose following their abortions, even though they were told they would feel "relief." Now, there was evidence to support the anxiety and distress they were feeling, and there was help for them through postabortion counseling, a service abortion clinics still refuse to recognize and provide.

There was finally a glimmer of light—hope for women who may have otherwise felt hopeless in the depression resulting from their past choices.

But what happens to a woman when her right to choose is determined by a schedule or influenced by a physician?

The next phase came in 2011, during the testimony of thousands of women who'd had abortions. It became evident that their decisions were not entirely voluntary.

Historically, it was presumed that a woman had already made up her mind before calling the abortion clinic, and the clinic just needed to schedule the procedure. In reality, women were really looking for someone to talk to so they could process their thoughts and questions. Too many women ended up in the assembly line, paid their money up front, signed the required forms, and went through with the abortion. They didn't see the doctor until they were in the procedure room, and by then it was too late to express their doubts.

Pro-choice advocates talk about not interfering with the "doctor-patient relationship." But where in this "assembly line" medicine does this exist? How is it even possible if the doctor doesn't live in your state? Who best counsels a woman—the abortion doctor, the abortion clinic personnel? Their opinions are guided by monetary goals or quotas, their personal convictions, and time constraints.

Who is truly interested in a pregnant woman's concerns, fears, and goals? Is her decision made without outside influences from the baby's father or her own family, or because of influences due to the woman's circumstances or religion, or her attention to celebrities, and so on? Is she given all the options, including resources in case she chooses to continue the pregnancy?

Considering all these factors, the South Dakota legislature in 2011 passed a new statute roughly called the Anti-Coercion Statute that was signed into law and immediately refuted by Planned Parenthood to keep from being enacted. Again, the law was appealed through the courts. Two of the three components are in effect at this writing. Only the section requiring counseling by a third party is still being litigated. The three sections of this statute require the following:

1. Only the medical doctor who will perform the abortion can assess for medical risk factors and obtain informed consent before the patient can schedule the abortion.

2. This personal contact by the physician must take place seventy-two hours prior to the abortion procedure, not counting weekends and holidays.

3. Options counseling, available resources should she [the woman] desire to continue the pregnancy, screening

and assessment of coercion, and other nonmedical questions must be obtained from a third party. This third party is a registered pregnancy help center of which there are two in South Dakota that fit the strict requirements of this law.

According to this law, these pregnancy help centers must fulfill the criteria and be registered by the state. Strict guidelines are imposed on what they can and cannot talk about as well as the training and licensing of the counselors. They must all be licensed and either social workers, counselors, psychologists, nurses, or family therapists. They discuss social issues, decision making, and resources, and screen for coercion (i.e., Are you being pressured or threatened? Do you feel safe?). They can't talk about medical procedures, medical risks of abortion, faith, or religion. Should the woman want to discuss those issues, she can make an appointment with a physician at another time.

During discussion in the South Dakota legislature on this bill protecting women seeking abortion, a solidly pro-choice abortion advocate said, "I think that as a legislative body, we should have a vested interest in making sure women get accurate information before they go through with any medical procedure." Amen, sister!

What is it like to be a mother of a unique child? Let's listen to the words from the mother of a thousand children, and arguably the most dedicated, sacrificial mother of all.

The following amicus brief was filed before the US Supreme Court (in the cases of Loce v. New Jersey and Krail et al. v. New Jersey) in February 1994 by Mother Teresa.[2] The letter addresses the 1973 court decision on Roe v. Wade establishing a legal right to abortion.

Robert George, Esq.
I hope you will count it no presumption that I seek your leave to address you on behalf of the unborn child. Like that child, I can be considered an outsider. I am not an American citizen. I was born before the First World War in a part of, what was not yet and is no longer, Yugoslavia. In many senses, I know what it is like to be without a country. When I was still a young girl, I traveled to India. I found my work among the poor and sick of that nation, and I have lived there ever since.

Since 1950, I have worked with my many sisters [almost 5,000 sisters, 400 foundations, in 100 countries] from around the world as one of the Missionaries of Charity. We care for those who are often treated as outsiders in their own communities by their own neighbors—the starving, the crippled, the impoverished, and the diseased, from the old woman with a brain tumor in Calcutta to the young man with AIDS in New York City. A special focus of our care is to mothers and their children. This includes mothers who feel pressured to sacrifice their unborn children by want, neglect, despair, and philosophical and government policies that promote the dehumanization of inconvenient human life. And it includes the children themselves—innocent and utterly defenseless, who are at the mercy of those who would deny their humanity.

So, in a sense, my sisters and those we serve are all outsiders together. At the same time, we are supremely conscious of the common bonds of humanity that unite us and transcend national boundaries. No one in the world who prizes liberty and human rights can feel anything but a strong kinship with America. Yours is the one great nation in all of history that was founded on the precept of equal rights and respect for all humankind, for the poorest and weakest of us as well as the richest and strongest. As your Declaration of Independence put it, in words that have never lost their power to stir the heart: "We hold these truths to be self-evident: that all men are created equal; that they are endowed by their creator with certain inalienable rights; that among these are life, liberty, and the pursuit of happiness . . ."

A nation founded on these principles holds a sacred trust: to stand as an example to the rest of the world, to climb ever higher in its practical realization of the ideas of human dignity, brotherhood, and mutual respect. Your constant efforts in fulfillment of that mission, far more than your size or wealth or military might, have made America an inspiration to all mankind . . . .

Yet, there has been [a] tragic and destructive departure from those American ideals in recent memory. It was this Court's own decision in Roe v. Wade (1973) to exclude the unborn child from the human family. You ruled that a mother, in consultation with her doctor, has broad discretion guaranteed against infringement by the United States Constitution, to choose to destroy her unborn child. Your opinion stated that you did not need to "resolve the difficult question of when life begins." That question is inescapable.

If the right to life is an inherent and inalienable right, it must surely exist wherever life exists. No one can deny that the unborn child is a distinct being, that it is human, and that it is alive. It is unjust, therefore, to deprive the unborn child of its fundamental right to life on the basis of its age, size, or condition of dependency. It was a sad infidelity to America's highest ideals when this Court said that it did not matter, or could not be determined when the inalienable right to life began for a child in its mother's womb.

America needs no words from me to see how your decision in Roe v. Wade has deformed a great nation. The so-called right to abortion has pitted mothers against their children and women against men. It has sown violence and discord at the heart of the most intimate human relationships. It has portrayed the greatest of gifts—a child—as a competitor, an intrusion, and an inconvenience. And in granting this unconscionable power [to the mother], it has exposed many women to unjust and selfish demands from their husbands or sexual partners.

Human rights are not a privilege conferred by government. They are every human being's entitlement

*by virtue of [their] humanity. The right to life does
not depend and must not be declared to be contingent
on the pleasure of anyone else, not even a parent or
a sovereign.*

*I have no new teaching for America. I seek only to
recall you to faithfulness to what you once taught the
world. Your nation was founded on the proposition—
very old as a moral precept, but startling and innovative
as a political insight—that human life is a gift of
immeasurable worth, and that it deserves, always
and everywhere, to be treated with the utmost dignity
and respect. I urge the Court to take the opportunity
presented by the petitions in these cases to consider the
fundamental question of when human life begins and
to declare without equivocation the inalienable rights
which it possesses.*

Leave it to a mother to say what's on her mind. Particularly when it comes to protecting her children. And it's not hard to believe that Mother Teresa must have felt that all children were related to her—to the same inextinguishable flame called the human race. This champion of life and great woman of faith wrote those convicting words decades ago, and here we are . . . still debating the issue.

It's impossible to deny that we're all special the moment we are created. We're all important from the beginning to the end. We're all treasured and precious in our own way, just as God crafted us to be. Each person is profoundly intentional. Entirely original. A unique human being.

A SAFE PLACE TO PONDER

"For you formed my inward parts;
you knitted me together in my mother's womb.
I praise you, for I am fearfully and wonderfully made."

PSALM 139:13-14

Dear Lord,

You make extraordinary things. That includes me. You designed everything about me. You numbered the hairs on my head. You provided all of my qualities—talent, ability, aptitude, insight, creativity, and vision. From conception to fruition, You brought me to life, and I ask that You help me to champion life wherever I find it.

In Jesus' name, amen.

CHAPTER TWELVE

MYTHS, RISKS, AND ONE LAST KISS

I am the way, and the truth, and the life.

JESUS OF NAZARETH

WHETHER OLD OR NEW, there's something compelling about a mythological story. Greek centaurs, the Himalayan yeti, and Scotland's Loch Ness monster all capture the imagination and take us to places unknown. We're thrilled by make-believe and enchanted by myth when we sit in a dark movie theater or read an enthralling novel.

But some myths have ambition—ambition to become truth.

Both sides of the abortion issue have their respective "truths and myths." But I prefer hard statistics and my own years in medicine as a guide to truth. Four top myths about abortion continue to mislead women.

Myths about Abortion

1. *It's just tissue.* A good friend of mine recently revealed to me she had an abortion when she was in college because the abortion clinic told her it was "just tissue." By the time she realized her mistake, years had passed. She kept this secret from her family, and her life has been overshadowed by guilt, shame, and anger for not being truly informed.

   It's now a codified South Dakota law that abortion ends the life of a separate unique human being, not "tissue." That law was based on a large body of scientific evidence and was confirmed by the Eighth Circuit Court. Closely tied to it is the question, When does life begin?

   In my mind, the serious question of when life begins has been irrevocably proven. Which leads us to the second myth about abortion.

2. *Legalizing abortion reduces maternal mortality.* This myth is difficult to reconcile because abortion and maternal mortality are not directly linked. It's comparing apples to oranges. In fact, the definitions of *pregnancy* and *mortality* are not even standardized. The World Health Organization uses nonmedical language and definitions, ratios where the denominators are not the same, and legal terms in lieu of medical terms. Therefore, their statistics and numbers are not helpful.

   The best evidence opposing this so-called fact

comes from Chile, where reliable records have been kept for decades. A report written by an epidemiologist, Dr. Elard Koch of the University of Chile, showed maternal mortality in Chile declined 93.8 percent, from 293.7 maternal deaths (per 100,000 live births) in 1960 to 18.2 maternal deaths in 2007.[1] Yet the highest mortality rate was in 1961 when abortion was legal. When the country made abortion illegal in 1989, the mortality rate dropped from 41.3 to 12.7 per 100,000 live births—a 69.2 percent decline. Therefore, this major improvement in maternal health is not related to access to legal abortion.

Three things account for Chile's drop in maternal mortality:

- Education of women (the key factor)
- Trained birth assistants to attend deliveries
- Triage of high-risk pregnant women to birth centers

Chile devoted resources to the development of highly trained personnel, the construction of many primary health centers, and the increase of schooling the population.

As a comparison, the neighboring South American country of Guyana at the same time liberalized its abortion laws and had the highest rate of maternal mortality. If legalizing abortion reduced mortality, then Guyana should have experienced mortality rates far below Chile's rates. But the opposite is true.

The third myth on our list is one that I've heard for years, which people continue to believe.

3. *Abortion is safer than childbirth.* An often-repeated, flawed report states that women are fourteen times more likely to die from childbirth than to die from abortion.[2] That report neglects to mention that eleven studies were excluded—scientific studies that adamantly disagreed with that statement. Those studies showed that death within 180 days of induced abortion is more than twice as high when compared with deaths within 180 days following childbirth.[3]

Finland is a country with single payer health care, universal access to health care, and exceptional data collection. Their seven-year study on nearly 10,000 women of reproductive age who had recently delivered, including postabortive women, showed that those who had an abortion were three and a half times more likely to die within a year compared with those who delivered at term. Additional stats revealed postabortive women were six times more likely to commit suicide.[4] The figures went on to show conclusively:

- Risk of death in a given year for a woman who had an abortion: 83 out of 100,000 ended pregnancies.
- Risk of death for a nonpregnant woman: 57 out of 100,000 ended pregnancies.
- Risk of death for women who miscarried: 52 out of 100,000 ended pregnancies.

- Risk of death for a pregnancy to term: 28 out of 100,000 ended pregnancies.

Unfortunately, it's not possible to compare numbers in US deaths from abortion and death related to childbirth due to incomplete reporting, voluntary collection of data, no consistency between states in birth and death certificates, and bias in reporting. On that subject, it should be said that reporting abortions to the Center for Disease Control is voluntary in America, and each state has its own rules and laws with little to no consistency.

The fourth and final myth I'd like to mention is possibly the most misleading and stigmatized one:

4. *Only women with mental health problems prior to abortion have mental problems after abortion.* Abortion is associated with a higher risk for negative psychological outcomes, especially when compared with other forms of perinatal loss and with unintended pregnancy carried to term.

Women with preexisting mental health problems are vulnerable and at increased risk of negative psychological reactions following an abortion. But all women undergoing abortion are at significant risk of depression, anxiety, substance abuse, suicidal ideation, and suicide.

There's a long list of universally accepted risk factors for women predisposed to adverse psychological problems following an abortion. Characteristics such as low self-esteem, ambivalence about the decision to abort, feeling pressured to have the abortion, intense guilt and shame, attachment to the baby or the pregnancy, believing abortion is murder, and others all contribute to mental health problems after an abortion. Even pro-choice organizations like the National Abortion Federation recognize these factors, although few (if any) abortion clinics address them in depth.

How do we help women facing a crisis—a decision that cannot be undone? How can we best serve women who feel they have no real choice and haven't truly processed their decision and might be looking for information?

To start with, better preabortion counseling and screening for these known psychological risk factors should be provided in every case. And as a society, we should be offering helpful information about available resources and support for women to continue their pregnancies if desired. Who knows how many of these mental health consequences could be prevented if women had accessible, tangible help?

The American Association of Pro-Life Obstetricians and Gynecologists began to publish their own studies since they were being denied by other medical publications. Once a board member myself, I approve of their mission statement and service: "Encourage and equip medical practitioners to provide an evidence-based rationale for defending the lives of both the pregnant mother and her unborn child."[5]

Yes, these myths have ambition. And if one is repeated often and loud enough, people will start to believe it—with or without the statistics to prove it. And that's dangerous because risks from abortion have physical and sometimes grave consequences. One such event in my years of treating women is still as fresh in my memory as if it happened yesterday. It's a day I would rather forget. Even though the following story is not about an abortion, it clearly illustrates the physical risks involved in one since abortions require the same type of skilled medical care as miscarriages do.

I was relaxing in front of the news on a Friday evening when the phone rang. The nurse on the other end sounded stressed as she asked if I was the OB-GYN doctor on call. When I said yes, she asked me to come to the hospital immediately for a nineteen-week miscarriage. Any second trimester procedure is inherently dangerous. Apparently, the local family doctor had started the D&C procedure, but the nurse wouldn't elaborate over the phone. Her tone was cautious as if the call was made privately and confidentially between us.

I found my way to the hospital and locker room to change into scrubs, then prepped for surgery. As I scrubbed my hands, I gazed through the window into the operating room. The patient was asleep, and the team was already transfusing blood in a pressure tourniquet for a quicker infusion. It wasn't a good sign.

As I entered the OR with my hands raised—keeping them sterile—I got on my gown and gloves. The other doctor was at the instrument table checking the tissue he had removed. At this point, I was on "autopilot," confident of my training but unsure of the controlled commotion unfolding in front of me.

Looking at the woman's condition and the excessive amount of bleeding, I thought the patient had a fifty-fifty chance of leaving the operating room alive. Any assertions I made in that OR were based on having performed thousands of abortions and hundreds of emergency D&Cs for miscarriages at all gestational ages. Blood was pouring out of her, and my professional supposition was that the patient's outcome could go either way.

Is the bleeding due to tissue still in the uterus, or from a laceration of the cervix, or from uterine perforation or . . . ? My mind rolled through all of the possible reasons for the hemorrhaging.

The British physicians I served with overseas talked about two kinds of bleeding: "troublesome ooze," which was definitely not the case with this patient, or "audible bleeding"— the sound of blood hitting the floor—which was applicable in this situation. I calmly sat down on the stool between the patient's legs that rested in the stirrups, and quickly began the examination.

"I hope she doesn't want any more children," I said out loud. By then, the uterus had been vigorously scraped. I couldn't feel any obvious disruption of the uterine wall, but time would tell if there had been a perforation.

The bleeding had now slowed considerably, and I instructed the anesthetist to start waking her up as I removed all the instruments and manually massaged the uterus. The patient's eyes flickered open, and I was relieved to see her awake.

Amazingly, she did well and after a couple of days, she went home. If it had been up to me, I would have watched her for another two days in the hospital for signs of infection or bowel obstruction in case there had been a uterine perforation. But her family doctor gave the green light, and her three children needed her care, so she was discharged.

Much later, as I got to know the OR nurse, she told me she feared for the patient's life. Turns out that patient had been seen earlier in the week by that same physician for minor bleeding at nineteen weeks. Over the next few days, the baby's heartbeat stopped, and the patient was then scheduled for a D&C that Friday afternoon following the doctor's clinic hours.

No one had called me in advance as a courtesy or asked me to scrub in for backup. I was there only because of a phone call from an insightful, vigilant nurse who got a sick feeling in the pit of her stomach. Thank God!

This kind of professional behavior is why the risks of abortion or D&C should be disclosed and openly discussed prior to the procedure. They cannot be understated or dismissed. They are real—and they can have life-altering and even life-ending consequences.

Risks of Abortion

The following undeniable risks of surgical abortion—though an incomplete list—can be divided into two categories: immediate and long-term. I wouldn't feel this book is complete without stating them.

Immediate Risks

1. *Direct injury to the cervix and/or uterus* leading to uterine perforation and possible serious injury to the

internal organs, such as the bowel, bladder, vascular arteries and veins—any of which can lead to death.

2. *Anesthesia complications*: a local cervical block, IV intravenous sedation, or the rarely used general anesthesia can cause an array of complications.

3. *Fainting or a vasovagal response* caused by stress, fear, or reaction to medicines can result in loss of consciousness.

4. *Bleeding and hemorrhage* are not uncommon and can be mild, moderate, or severe, and are the result of direct injury or retained tissue in the uterus.

5. *Retained tissue* left in the uterus can cause bleeding, infection, and the necessity of a second procedure which, when done right away, lessens the long-term complications.

6. *Infection* can be caused by an undiagnosed sexually transmitted disease, inadequate cleansing of the vaginal area, a breach in sterile technique, or insufficient sterilization of equipment.

7. *Lack of medical follow-up and postabortion complications:* Abortion clinics are reluctant to acknowledge these risks and complications, and unfortunately, some patients are sent home without addressing problems. Once released, patients end up calling an ambulance or going to the hospital where the ER doctors are unfamiliar with what was done, if in fact the patient even reveals she's had an abortion. Abortion doctors are not always from the community or don't

have admitting privileges at the local hospital, therefore any problems are not reported back to or followed up by the abortion clinic. Out-of-town patients may travel long distances and their transportation can create problems. For example, blood clots can form when the patient is sitting in a car for hours.

Long-term Risks

1. *Preterm delivery or preterm birth* (PTD)/PTB) among pregnancies following an abortion is well known as a risk of elective, induced abortion. And the risk of preterm birth increases with each additional abortion— 25 percent increased risk of PTB after one abortion; 32 percent increased risk after more than one abortion; 51 percent increased risk of PTB after more than two abortions.

2. *Incompetent cervix*: This happens when the cervix is weakened or damaged with the manual dilation (opening of the cervix) during the procedure—especially if it's beyond the necessary dilation. The manual dilation may cause direct trauma, such as tears, or simply weaken the cervix in subsequent pregnancies. If the incompetent cervix is diagnosed early in a pregnancy, a procedure that puts a stitch in the cervix can help. However, patients often are unwilling to divulge that they've had an abortion even when it's legal, and the risk goes unrecognized.

3. *Asherman's Syndrome* can be caused anytime the inside of the uterus is instrumented, such as when the uterus

is scraped and suctioned during an abortion. Any overaggressive scraping can cause scar tissue to form in the uterine lining that may result in infertility. The embryo may not be able to implant (insert itself in the uterine tissue). Or the placenta may abnormally attach, as in placenta previa when the placenta is in front of the baby. Placenta previa requires a C-section delivery and may cause serious hemorrhaging.

4. *Depression, suicidal thoughts, and suicide*: A careful, large meta-analysis in 2011 revealed that abortion is a significant risk factor for mental health problems.[6] Feelings such as grief, loss, depression, and alienation from others can occur following abortion.

5. *Breast cancer association*: We know that delivering a baby full term has a protective effect on the breast, and the protection increases with the birth of more children. There is some literature suggesting a possible link between elective abortion and increased risk of developing breast cancer. One theory is that the sudden withdrawal of pregnancy hormones after an abortion affects the breast tissue.

Risks of Medical Abortions

Medical abortions can also cause potential complications, and their use has been steadily increasing since 2000. Currently, medical abortions are approved up to seventy days confirmed by ultrasound. A medical abortion is a procedure using medication to end a pregnancy. No surgery or anesthesia is required.

Two medications are used: A woman takes the first in the clinic and the second medication later at home. Even though every woman undergoing a medical abortion experiences cramping and heavy bleeding, the bleeding can be severe and become a hemorrhage requiring a blood transfusion. Eight percent of medical abortions require surgical completion due to this bleeding or because of incomplete passage of tissue. Adding to the risk is the fact that some women take the first abortion medication but change their minds and don't take the second home medication.

There does exist an "abortion pill rescue" process that salvages some of these pregnancies. This is done under the supervision of a medical doctor, and its success rate has yet to be determined.[7]

Now you know the dangerous risks of abortion and the myths without merit. Armed with this knowledge, women can make educated, sound, and safe decisions that will directly affect their health physically, mentally, and emotionally. And though some things are difficult to hear, I prefer to have all the information I need in order to reach the best conclusion.

One Last Kiss

The word *hospice* brings up all kinds of images of service, suffering, and tearful farewells. But preface it with the word *perinatal*, and the word is sadder still.

Hospice care initially seems to be an unfair and strange thing in the context of a tiny life that has yet to take a first breath. Parents are forced to ponder the fatal diagnosis of their unborn baby. They're told that the child won't live long once he or she leaves the protection of the womb, but they don't know whether their infant will live for a day, a week, or a month. They do know that their relationship will be brief, and they wonder if it's worth the unconscionable anguish of seeing the pregnancy through. So they're left with a heart-wrenching decision: to either carry the baby to term or terminate their child's life.

When abortion became legal, it was a common reaction to assume that termination of the pregnancy was the best option when a severe abnormality of the baby was discovered in utero. Some doctors would assume this was the only reasonable option. The rush to end the pregnancy didn't come from lack of compassion, but perhaps from a desire to have something to offer the grieving couple and to spare them more distress than necessary—to allow them to just "get it over with."

As technology improved, ultrasound and other methods for early diagnosis of fetal anomalies that were "not compatible with life" were discovered. At the same time in Britain, the concept of adult hospice was developed in the 1990s. Many of us have had experience with an adult in their final stages of care.

At the beginning of the twenty-first century, using the adult model, caring doctors, nurses, social workers, and others developed the concept of perinatal hospice. They established a multidisciplinary, comprehensive team approach to provide a model of care that incorporates the strengths of early diagnosis, management of grief, and hospice care to address the needs of families losing an infant.[8]

How do these couples make such a difficult choice between ending a pregnancy or carrying the baby to term? And what happens if they decide to keep the baby, knowing the inevitable outcome? What are the legal guidelines within the shadow of such an awful event?

In my state of South Dakota (as perhaps all states), the Department of Public Health Vital Records division requires that a baby with any sign of life, no matter how small, must have a birth certificate issued. If the infant dies, this requires a fetal death report, which is akin to a death certificate. In addition to this, any parent may provide a name for a stillborn child upon requesting a certificate of birth resulting in stillbirth. If the parent doesn't wish to provide a name, the Department of Health will fill in the certification with the name "baby boy" or "baby girl" and the last name of the parent.

That process leads the parent(s) to a law specifying options for dealing with the remains: medical incineration, cremation, or burial. Any stillbirth at twenty completed weeks or more will need a fetal death report, and the remains cannot be incinerated. The stillborn baby must have cremation or burial, which includes a burial permit and transit for the funeral director.

If all of this feels a bit detached and surreal to you, you're not alone. Many parents have been forced to make these decisions for decades, in the midst of their grief. It's difficult to read about them much less contemplate the options in a personal way. But I'd like to share a story showing why a couple would choose to carry a baby to term and deal with all of these details.

Lacy and Mason had a choice to make. At their twenty-week ultrasound, their baby received a terminal diagnosis, a condition caused by a chromosome abnormality. Shock and sorrow set in as they were asked when they would like to schedule the abortion—as if it were the only option. It was a question they couldn't answer. The car ride home was as silent as their tears.

Their two young healthy sons were excited about the prospect of having a little sister, and the family's happy impatience had been growing as the months went on. But now with this devastating prognosis came an unthinkable dilemma: *What should we do for our child who is incurable?*

Late into the night, the couple talked about what it all meant—to carry a baby so quickly bound for heaven. How people, coworkers, and friends would react to the news, and could they handle the decision to keep the baby for as long as the Lord allowed? Or should they spare their living children, family members, and their own aching hearts the sting of losing someone they could never keep?

But they had already given her a name. *Lilly.*

She was already loved, cherished, adored though hidden away in a tender, safe place only God could create. Her bedroom was almost ready with puffy clouds and sun-drenched angels half-painted on the ceiling. A crib with a new coat of enamel dried to a shiny white and was filled with soft, cozy stuffed animals. Her stroller, a hand-me-down from the boys, was refitted with pink wheels and a quilted flower lining.

The thought of aborting their daughter was more than

Lacy and Mason could bear. So the next morning, the young parents chose to keep their girl until the hour of her natural departure. They gathered their boys and tenderly told them that their baby sister would be a visitor for only a short while.

The children's faces wrestled with the puzzling idea.

"Why can't we keep her? Don't you love Lilly enough to let her stay?" one child said as his eyes shimmered.

"It's not that we don't love her, Bud. It's that God loves her more, and He can't live without her for very long," Lacy said, almost believing it herself.

"Can we say good-bye to her?" his brother asked with a glimmer of hope.

"If you're sure you want to," Mason agreed. "You both can."

It was decided.

In the hospital, precious Lilly entered the world. Her fragile limbs seemed rosy and perfect, though her eyes never opened. Yet she had to have known she wasn't alone. Both of her brothers held her and caressed her head of wispy curls. Grandma and Grandpa Park, and Nanna and Papa Miller were there too, each taking their turn to cradle the tiny infant.

Mason rested Lilly on her mother's breaking heart as both parents pressed their lips to her velvety skin. One hour later, Lilly went home to be with the Lord.

She left her family rich with memories and mementos: a yellow baby blanket, a hospital ID bracelet, a lock of hair, hand and footprints in tiny puddles of impressionable clay. And most of all, they have the everlasting treasure of their final memory—a loving farewell . . . and one last kiss.

A SAFE PLACE TO PONDER

"Your eyes have seen my formless substance;
and in Your book were written all the days that were
ordained *for me*, when as yet there was not one of them."

PSALM 139:16, NASB

Dear Jesus,

*Life is so precious in every form, every time, in every
person. In the hidden places as well as the stark light of
our short visit, only You know how many hours have been
predestined for us. Give me a renewed sense of respect
for those valuable moments here.*

In Jesus' name, amen.

CHAPTER THIRTEEN

WHAT MIGHT HAVE BEEN

Yesterday, all my troubles seemed so far away.
Now it looks as though they're here to stay. Oh, I believe in yesterday.
JOHN LENNON AND PAUL MCCARTNEY

PINK FRECKLES DOTTED HER FACE—too many to count—yet placed there lovingly by a God who adores diversity in the extreme. Another patient had black hair cascading over shoulders weathered by the desert sun. A never-ending succession of women came through my office—both in the United States and overseas. They were all special, distinct, troubled.

With the number of patients I've treated over the years, my investment is still limited compared with the multitude of women who walk into hospitals, clinics, and urgent care facilities every minute across the globe. With so many stories to tell, I sometimes wonder what might have been. How many lives could have been saved if only . . . *if only.*

They say truth is stranger than fiction, and taking into

account what I've seen, I have to agree. But for argument's sake, let's look at a young woman who could be anyone you know—your daughter, sister, friend, coworker, neighbor. She's a character I dreamed up, but I've seen her walk through my door more times than I can say. And ultimately, the decision she makes cannot be undone. But *what if* she could see into the future? How many scenarios would it take to find the best solution for her? Let's look at three.

Sour stomach. Late period. Anxiety rising.

Alex had just turned twenty-one when she got a positive sign on her pregnancy test. None of her friends had ever been stupid enough to get into this situation (that she knew of), and her mother and father would never look at their little girl the same way again. Her mom would tell her to keep the baby, maybe give it up for adoption. Her dad would be livid, then devastated. Her on-again, off-again boyfriend, Kyle, just packed his stuff and left, and she was barely making the rent.

There she was, without the money or means to raise a child, and no one to help her figure it out. She would have to make the decision on her own.

Choice #1: There's Nothing to Say

Her bare legs dangled from the exam table as she wiped her sweaty palms on the paper gown. Alex felt vulnerable enough without thinking about the moral and emotional impact of her decision. There was really nothing to say; she would have the abortion and then move on with her life like nothing had happened. Lots of girls do it, and you can't identify one of them out on the street. No damage done. She just wanted to get back to normal the quickest and easiest way possible.

"I'm not married, I don't have a boyfriend, and I'm broke," she told the doctor. "There's just no other option for me." Her words came out in a rush.

"You're a grown woman, and you have the right to terminate this pregnancy," Dr. Sweet said. "It's a short procedure, but you'll need a driver. We use a general anesthesia at this clinic, so you'll be out during the procedure and won't remember a thing."

"That's perfect."

That meant Alex would have to recruit someone—a very understanding, nonjudgmental someone—to shuttle her to and from the appointment. *Beth would do it.* She was by far Alex's most progressive-thinking friend, a little older with an impressive resume of life experience. Beth was sure to be a sympathetic yet objective witness. Exactly what Alex needed.

"Does anyone else have to know?" Alex couldn't help asking.

"No, this is purely confidential. It's your life. Your body. Your choice." The doctor's soothing tone was hypnotizing, as if she had given this speech many times before, as if there was no other truth out there, as if an abortion was the best and safest thing to do.

Alex's shoulders suddenly relaxed. Everything was going to be fine.

"Thanks, Doc."

"Since you're only six weeks along, we'll wait another month, just to make sure we get everything."

"Okay," Alex replied, "see you next month."

"The front desk will make the appointment for you, Alex," Dr. Sweet said as she peeled off her latex gloves and left the room.

Four more weeks of dealing with morning sickness, bloated belly, sore breasts, making up excuses as to why her cheeks looked so flushed and clammy. This would be the longest month of her life.

Her life. That's what mattered. She wasn't going to think twice about aborting a cluster of cells that had no soul. She just didn't believe it was alive. And she didn't want anyone to change her mind.

A week passed, then another, and another. Finally, the day came when Alex and Beth sat in the clinic waiting room. It was busy with lots of women of all ages, reading magazines, talking to their designated drivers. Some seemed to be completely at ease while others looked terrified and tearful.

Alex was somewhere in between. The trick was not to think about it at all, to act like this was a trip to the dentist—unpleasant but necessary. A few minutes went by as a couple of women were called back behind the doors that Alex mused was a time machine. Walk through those doors, and you leap ahead to a future that looks exactly the way you left it before being so careless. Don't walk through them, and you're trapped in the impossible present where your power is lost and your ability to do *what* you want, *when* you want, and *how* you want is gone. Life as you once knew it would be over.

"Alex!" A voice caught her off guard.

She glanced at Beth who was staring at her phone. "I'll see you in a bit," her friend said with a casual smile.

In the exam room, Alex closed her eyes and counted backwards from 100 . . . "99, 98, 97 . . ." Lights out.

A second later, she woke up groggy and relieved. It was all over.

"Don't overdo it for the next few days," the recovery nurse warned. "Then you can go back to your normal activities."

The first couple of days, Alex declined a surprising invitation to go horseback riding with her ex-boyfriend, Kyle, and also a jog with a coworker after her shift. She took things easy. On the third day, she returned to her usual high-voltage schedule: lunch, then shopping all afternoon with a friend, followed by an errand to pick up flowerpots and soil at Grey's Garden Center for her mom before meeting her for dinner. Alex was on course again, without anyone finding out about her detour.

Opting for outdoor seating at their favorite fish and chips place, Alex and her mother chatted over panko-breaded salmon. But her mom noticed something about her daughter, something a little off.

"Why are you so pale? You feel okay, Sweetie?"

"I'm going to pop into the little girl's room for a minute, Mom. Be right back!" Alex said, doing her best to shield any concern as she ducked into the restaurant.

The restroom started to spin as her heart rate skipped like a needle on a vinyl record. And it only got worse the longer she sat in the stall—the roll of toilet paper was dwindling. Alex was bleeding. Badly. Panic set in as she thought about how she would explain her condition to her unsuspecting mother.

"Alex, are you in here?" her mother's worried voice called out.

"Mom, I need you!" She couldn't bear to say it, but it was true. She was in trouble.

Unlatching the stall door, Alex reluctantly let in her mom, who stared down at her in horror.

"Alex . . . what's happening?"

"I had an abortion three days ago," Alex replied like a frightened child. "I couldn't tell you," she said, looking everywhere but at her mother's face. "Please do something."

One ambulance ride later, Alex was given a shot to control the bleeding and was back on the table for a D&C. She had lied to her mom, acted without considering all of the consequences, and put her life in jeopardy. And that was only what the naked eye could see.

Given another chance, she would have done things differently.

Choice #2: I Can't Take It Back

The white paper gown made Alex's legs look tanner than they really were.

"I'm not married, I don't have a boyfriend, and I'm broke. There's no way I can tell my parents. They've always preached abstinence, and I think it would kill them if they found out I wasn't a virgin. Sorry— I'm just confused."

"You're a grown woman, and you have the right to do what's best for you. You can keep the baby or terminate the pregnancy," Dr. Sweet said with confidence.

"Does anyone else have to know?"

"It's strictly confidential. It's your life. Your body. Your choice."

"I just don't see any other way—," Alex's voice trailed off. The word *terminate* left her breathless. It was a negative word—not passive or harmless, but destructive. Even violent.

"It's a short procedure, but you'll need a driver. We use a general anesthesia at this clinic, so you'll be out during the procedure and won't remember a thing."

"I guess. I mean, yes. Okay." What else could she say without another clear choice?

When the day came, Alex sat in the waiting room with Beth. Her chest was pounding, like when she broke her leg on a mountaintop while skiing. She'd felt helpless then too. Her eyes followed the sweeping secondhand of the clock on the clinic's wall. It moved so slowly, Alex thought it was broken—like her leg had been, like her life was now. Her hands shook as she pulled a derelict strand of hair away from her hot face.

"Alex!" a nurse's voice rang out.

She glanced at Beth who was staring at her phone. "I'll see you in a bit."

In the exam room, Alex counted backwards from 100 . . . "99, 98, 97 . . ." How would she feel when she woke up?

A second later, her eyes opened, and she realized she was crying.

"That's just a side effect from the anesthesia, Alex. You're okay," the nurse reassured her. "Don't overdo it for the next few days. Then you can resume your normal activities."

That week, Alex stayed in bed. When her silenced cell phone buzzed, she convinced her mother and her employer that she was just feeling under the weather. And it was true—in every way—she felt sick.

Was there something else she could have done? Confided in her mom who loved her and always gave her the best advice? Talked about it with a sympathetic friend to discuss any options that she may have overlooked? Prayed about it? But it was too late for that now.

Twenty years later, Alex wept as she sank into the couch of her church counselor. She couldn't understand why she was so anxious and angry. Everything made her mad: the jerk who cut her off in traffic, the slow-moving cashier at the checkout counter, the child who wouldn't stop crying in the coffee shop. No matter what it was, Alex reacted in the same irrational way—an uncontrolled inner explosion, like a lit stick of dynamite she couldn't stomp out.

But her counselor amazed her with a single, sensible sentence.

"Alex, you have every reason to be angry."

"What do you mean?" Alex couldn't adjust to the thought. "No, I don't."

"You were twenty-one years old, and never given an option to that abortion. So now you strike out at everyone because you can't take it back. You're furious and you should be."

"But what can I do about it now? It's too late!" Alex shut her eyes to quell the flowing stream of remorse. "I'll never be able to say I'm sorry."

Her counselor took her hand and gave it a mild squeeze. "Of course you will. Your child is in heaven right now, waiting for you. And when you get there, you'll meet her, and hug her, and tell her everything that's on your heart."

"But what if she hates me?" Alex couldn't imagine it any other way. "Why wouldn't she hate me?"

"She doesn't hate you, Alex. She loves you. And you can tell her how much you love her when you see her."

If that little piece of wisdom was supposed to make Alex stop crying, it didn't work. Her tears fell harder as if trying to wash off two decades of shame. But it *did* explain her pain, hostility, and low self-esteem. And though she couldn't take back what she had done, now she could move forward in forgiving herself. She could let God begin to heal her present to make a way for a healthier, happier future.

Fear, resentment, sadness: They were all results of a decision made years before. As Alex dried her tears, she wondered what her life would have looked like had she taken another road. If only she had another chance.

Choice #3: There Are Always Other Options

Alex already had a game plan. She would terminate the pregnancy—as much as she hated the word *terminate*—and move on.

"You're a grown woman, and you have the right to a safe, legal abortion," Dr. Sweet insisted.

"I don't have any other option. I can't tell my parents; they'd never speak to me again."

"Are you sure about that?" Suddenly, Dr. Sweet switched gears, and Alex's plan hit a snag.

"No," Alex had to admit. "They're very loving, nurturing people. But how can I break it to them that their virgin daughter is pregnant? And I don't think the 'immaculate conception' story is gonna work for me. Although, I've never challenged them on why my birthday and their anniversary fall exactly nine months apart."

"We've all been young," the doctor said. "There are other options besides abortion. Carry to term and give up the baby for adoption. Or you could keep it, with the help of your parents or partner. But whatever you do, Alex, you don't have to do it alone."

But Alex was good at being alone. Her life was all mapped out. She had goals and dreams, and none of them included a baby. But why was a child such a bad thing? It could bring her stability. A new relationship with her mom and dad. Who knows? Once they got past their disappointment in her, they'd realize their first grandchild was on the way. Maybe she could even mend her broken love affair—some guys adore kids, and Kyle might be one of them. And as the father, didn't he have a say in the matter?

Alex started to squirm; she wasn't convinced that their breakup was all Kyle's fault. Now that she thought about it, she had thrown him out for making her laugh too much.

"Every girl should have your problem, Alex," Beth had said when she'd heard the frustration in her friend's voice about the man whose main objective was to make her smile.

Dr. Sweet wheeled her stool a bit closer. "Why don't you have a talk with your support group—anyone you trust and believe has your best interest at heart. And then make a decision you can live with."

The doctor was making way too much sense.

"Okay." Alex couldn't believe she was actually giving the

matter a second thought. But the doctor was right. There was more to say. There were conversations she needed to have. In the end, whatever Alex did, she couldn't take it back.

"I'll talk to Kyle, then my mom. I'll let *her* talk to my dad, God help us."

To Alex's astonishment, she had options that could turn out to be a blessing in disguise.

———————

As women, we tend to think ahead, to manufacture multiple ways a situation can unfold—for good or not-so-good. Usually, we fixate on the not-so-good possibilities, probably because we don't have the luxury of making mistakes. Right or wrong, many of us feel small, weak, of little value, and at odds with our surroundings. But our imagination can give us great insight and opportunity if we only let it.

No matter what happens to us in life, there's a universal law: An action requires a reaction. Doing something or nothing at all—both are a response. Sometimes we have only a split second to decide how to best respond. But most of the time, there is space, a place to exhale, think, pray, talk, choose, find peace. And if you look around, there's always another option.

To find the best solution, use that incredible gift of creative vision and your connection to God who sees your every circumstance before it arrives. Think of the many ways to adapt and respond to your present situation.

Save yourself from having to wonder *what might have been.*

A SAFE PLACE TO PONDER

"Where there is no guidance, a people falls,
but in an abundance of counselors there is safety."

PROVERBS 11:14

Lord Jesus,

There will be times when I'm faced with a difficult decision that frightens me—that makes me feel alone and out of control. But if I humble myself before You, and seek wise counsel of those I trust, then I'm never really alone. You and Your servants are there to help me through it. Thank You for taking the fear out of the future, and the question mark from what might have been.

In Your name, amen.

CHAPTER FOURTEEN

IN SOLIDARITY OF LIFE

I once was lost but now am found; was blind but now I see.

JOHN NEWTON

FROM THE BEGINNING OF our search for truth, to the beginning of our life in Jesus Christ and beyond, God leads us through the uncompromising wine press of experience so we can become rich, fragrant, and full of character, producing a sweet aroma that will last throughout eternity.

I think about that little girl who was carelessly forgotten one afternoon, left at home all alone, only to be found again. I contemplate my upbringing, education, first love and marriage, divorce, and another marriage. I studied, worked hard, gained and lost—another husband, a job, my identity. I treasured life while at the same time taking life without apology. My pro bono efforts overseas and the letters from strangers who waited patiently for me to return—letters that would shape my path and future assignments—were an integral part of God's divine plan for me.

What changed me? Was it people carrying around disturbing photos of abortions just to make a point? The anti-abortion zealots calling me names and threatening my life? Was it the activists loitering outside my clinic, yelling hate through the window? That couldn't be the reason because the more they tried to stop me, the more determined I was to continue. But God was there, too, churning the winepress, using these experiences to empty me of myself so He could fill me with His Spirit.

He appointed a nun to pray for me in secret because she read an article and saw a spark of hope. So she fanned that spark for the next ten years. He placed warriors in my way to disarm me and draw me closer to the Kingdom they were defending. He gave me a voice and commissioned me to spread the gospel of life. He provided a platform to reach millions and has continued that commission through this book and transparent activism.

As I started to investigate the hard questions and thoughtfully consider various opinions about protecting life and the consequences of what I had done, everything I believed slowly collapsed. Perhaps I wasn't saving women's lives after all, and all of the babies who lost their lives by the work of my hands represented a terrible mistake—my mistake.

I eventually found that line in the sand in my own heart. I didn't find it on a stilted fact sheet or in an annual report, but as I listened to the Holy Spirit's voice, which grew louder as my faith reached out to its author.

"But God" are two of my favorite words in the Bible.

They prove that God has complete control no matter what is happening around us. He has always had His own program, plans, and promises that still echo throughout His Word:

> "*But God* shows his love for us in that while we were still sinners . . ." (Romans 5:8). "*But God* was with him and rescued him out of all his afflictions" (Acts 7:9-10). "*But God* knows your hearts" (Luke 16:15). "*But God* raised him from the dead" (Acts 13:30). "*But God* has called us to peace" (1 Corinthians 7:15, NASB). "*But God* had mercy on him [and her]" (Philippians 2:27). [italics mine]

But God . . . sent His Son, Jesus, for us.

Jesus is the true Vine, committed to our full development, and we are the thirsty branches drinking deep of His love. And just as God promised, He will complete what He started in us. From beginning to beginning, He is faithful.

I wish I could tell you what you want to hear: that abortion and other man-made destruction will soon be stifled and ended once and for all. But I doubt abortion will end—not now, maybe never. What I can tell you is that people are hurting and in need of hope, and the answer to that lack of hope can be found in Scripture.

Joel 2:13 tells us, "Return to the LORD your God, for he is gracious and merciful, slow to anger, and abounding in steadfast love." That statement calms me. But before we can return to God, we are humbled and weakened (by the enemy God allows in) beyond our abilities to cope alone. Then we return to God of our own free will. And when we have endured the season that has ground us to dust, God promises in Joel 2:25 that He "will restore to you the years that the swarming locust has eaten." In me, God restored peace, compassion, forgiveness—all those qualities that are the hallmark of His workmanship.

If we will only turn to God in our struggles, He will be gracious, forbearing, and kind to us. No matter how sour the fruit of our careless errors, He will make us suitable for heavenly service. It's His pleasure, His joy, to bring us ever closer to our original design and intimate relationship with Him.

After a lifetime of mistakes and deliverance from them, I can say forthrightly and without a doubt that no one is beyond redemption. No matter what you've done or failed to do, all is not lost. Our divine Redeemer is on your side, and He will make all things work together for good.

The blemishes and bruises from daily battering, along with our blind direction and the unwitting damage we've done to fellow human beings, big or small, in no way steal us from God's reach. In our achievements and victories, Jesus is with us. In our darkest hour and greatest need, He is there. And there is nothing you can do to stop Him from loving you. No mental lapse, no uninformed choice, no act of cruelty can make Him turn away from you. He is irreversibly invested because you are His. You were made *for* Him, and *through* Him, and *in* Him, and *by* Him you will finally return to Him—or not. It's one more very important choice for you to make. God is in everything, whether you believe and cleave to that faith—the ultimate source of perfect redemption—or refuse and continue in your own limited logic and strength. He is still there.

History is a well of inspiration that reminds me of those who have previously traveled my way, if not in my shoes. Oliver Wendell Holmes Sr. first trained to be a doctor in Paris at various prestigious medical schools. He then moved home to Massachusetts to acquire his doctor of medicine degree from Harvard Medical School in 1836. But it seems his inner poet couldn't be denied, and he was acclaimed by his fellow Fireside Poets such as Ralph Waldo Emerson and Henry Longfellow as one of the best writers of his day.

As a well-known medical reformer, author, professor, lecturer, and inventor, Holmes wrote: "I find the great thing in this world is not so much where we stand, as in what direction we are moving: To reach the port of heaven, we must sail sometimes with the wind and sometimes against it, but we must sail, and not drift nor lie at anchor." [1]

That sentiment resonates with me: We need movement in our daily spiritual walk instead of stagnation. We need to lay hold of God's promise to transform us into the image of His Son. God, our moral and spiritual motivator, should be our defining goal. How easy it is to lose sight of our forward progress as we look down, dredging the bottom of our own compassless bay in hopes of finding divine treasure—something eternal that rust will not destroy and thieves cannot steal. Something bigger than ourselves.

But we forget, more quickly than we admit, that our mission should remain a humane effort to educate and illuminate others. To gently reveal the goodness of God with tender, convicting instruction, which can only be successfully wrought by the all-consuming power of the Holy Spirit. In Him, there is no need to fight.

Through prayer and petition, with thanksgiving, the way is made clear to us. And through us, God will lead others to the spoils of a battle Christ has already won. We are commanded to pray, put on the armor, and to stand! We proclaim God's sovereignty in all things, praise His audacious grace, and believe in faith that what He has set out to accomplish no one or thing can thwart. His Word is final. Despite what mankind does or refuses to do, God's divine purpose will be fulfilled.

Having been a part of the abortion industry, the green bottom line is hard to ignore. In this country, it has become commerce—abortion on demand has become a common form of marketable birth control. With the baby's point of viability moving earlier and earlier in pregnancy, at what day/week do we protect the life of the child?

My heart and passion as an OB-GYN doctor is to protect the lives of both of my patients at every stage. Many who rally for pro-choice are fearful that things will go back to the days before Roe v. Wade, but we are not in those times anymore—socially or technologically.

Back in the day, a nonmarried pregnant woman faced degradation and misery, especially if she was a working woman who couldn't hide away. The stigma of being an unwed mother is certainly not a problem now. If anything, it shows admirable strength and fortitude to take on single motherhood. In fact, the vast majority of pregnant women in this country are unmarried, in stable and monogamous relationships, and simply don't feel nuptials are necessary.

Contemporary changes in obstetrics since 1973, such as the modern ultrasound machine, have upgraded our vision from a snowstorm to high resolution with optics more complex than our ability to interpret them. The window into the womb has a 3D and 4D clarity that shows movement, kicking, smiling, eyes opening and closing. In the old days, we couldn't always identify the gender of the baby. Now, doctors can email a sharp, animated snapshot of the boy or girl to their patient's iPhone.

It's truly a new day.

When I was performing abortions, I never second-guessed the annual figures I received regarding women dying from illegal abortion. Today, I know more than ever that they were grossly padded in order to sway public opinion before the issue made its way to the Supreme Court in 1973. But whether the calculations seem correct or not, we're left with one final thing to reconcile: Life, no matter how small, deserves protection.

Abortion is not the panacea we originally thought it was. There are no longer any noble reasons for resorting to it. And we now recognize the risks and residual effects that abortion creates. It's been several decades since Roe v. Wade was passed. It's time that we acknowledge a new dawn, and in the light of that rising sun, we can offer options, support, and encouragement to women who are confused about the direction they should go.

As long as there are those of us who are willing, it should

be our joy and privilege to take others by the hand in healing solidarity of life—all life.

A SAFE PLACE TO PONDER

"It was fitting to celebrate and be glad, for this your [sister] was dead, and is alive again; [she] was lost, and is found."

LUKE 15:32

Jesus,

My lovely Friend and Savior, thank You for blessing me with a spirit of patience, forgiveness, and healing. Forgive me for offending You. Redeem me from my past and ordain me for future works of service. Give me the words that support life while loving those who would sooner take that life. Help me to make a lasting difference in the women around me who might be struggling with that decision.

In Your name, amen.

ACKNOWLEDGMENTS

To my Abba Father, glorious Lord, who never gave up on me. You picked me up from the pit I was in, forgave me all my sins, and remember them no more. You showed me my purpose—to speak out for life. And every time I wanted to give up on this project, You wouldn't let me. Instead, You sent me angels, without which this book would still be on scraps of paper tossed in a box.

Leslee Unruh, you are an extraordinary friend. All you have done and continue to do is far more than a ministry. Your strength, courage, caring, determination, not to mention your polished style and enthusiasm for living, have impacted me since the day we met. Your love of God, your passion for people, and boundless energy fuels your desire to help. And you have helped me more than you know.

Kimberly Shumate, it is truly one of God's miracles how we came to work together. You are the perfect balance of taskmaster, patient collaborator, writer extraordinaire, and great fun to work with. I trusted your judgment and experience completely, and I'm so thankful I did.

And my gratitude goes out to the many people who prayed for me over the years, including Sister Josita Schwab and her fervent daily intercession for a nonbeliever whom she didn't even know. I thank God for her passion for prayer, and for picking me from a newspaper article to direct her petitions to God on my behalf. Also, thank you to the prayer team and army of servants at the Alpha Center in Sioux Falls, who have consistently covered me with prayer. May God bless you mightily for your patience and persistence.

And to Dr. Rebecca as well as so many others who I haven't met but have carried a burden to pray for me for years. Those prayers are cherished, and I hope to meet you someday. If not in this life, then the one that is to come.

Thank you to my friends David and Margaret Houck for your encouraging words. Over the years, you have continued to urge me to share my story, and I thank God for your faithfulness, friendship, and many musical talents that uplift those around you.

True acknowledgment also goes to Roger and Sharon Hunt who tirelessly and humbly fought for the rights of the unborn. Much of the South Dakota legislation is due to their courage and steadfast work. Sadly, we lost this quiet couple, but their memory lives on.

To Larry Weeden and the team at Focus on the Family and Tyndale House Publishers who were willing to publish this book, thank you. I appreciate you all and hope our efforts will touch many lives.

Finally, thank you, Mom. Though you already had your hands full with three young children—one with special needs—you chose to give me life. You were a special woman, and I miss you every day and look forward to seeing you again in heaven.

NOTES

CHAPTER 3: THE SEPTIC TANK
1. Sarah Kliff, "The Gosnell Case: Here's What You Need to Know," *Washington Post*, April 15, 2013.
2. Joe Stumpe and Monica Davey, "Abortion Doctor Shot to Death in Kansas Church," *New York Times*, May 31, 2009.
3. John Joseph Powell, *The Secret of Staying in Love,* reprint ed. (Thomas More Press, 1995).

CHAPTER 5: IT'S COMPLICATED
1. Terry Sollom, "State Actions on Reproductive Health Issues in 1996," *Perspectives on Sexual and Reproductive Health* 27, no. 1 (January/February 1997), www.guttmacher.org/journals/psrh/1997/01/state-actions-reproductive -health-issues-1996.
2. William Booth, "Doctor Killed during Abortion Protest," *Washington Post*, March 11, 1993.
3. Stumpe and Davey, "Abortion Doctor Shot to Death in Kansas Church."
4. Jim Yardley and David Rohde, "Abortion Doctor in Buffalo Slain," *New York Times*, October 25, 1998.

CHAPTER 7: THE PRAYER OF SISTER JOSITA
1. Monica Davey, "National Battle over Abortion Focuses on South Dakota Vote," *New York Times*, November 1, 2006.

CHAPTER 8: JUST LIKE ME
1. For more information, I hope you'll visit alphacenter.org and alphacenter friends.org.

2. Derek Prince, *The Grace of Yielding* (New Kensington, PA: Whitaker House, 1977).
3. "The Abortion Doctor," published Oct 25, 2008, YouTube video, 6:10, https://www.youtube.com/watch?v=wZqbPtWgqu4.

CHAPTER 9: IT'S A PRAYER MEETING, NOT A PROTEST

1. "The Call Nashville, Dr. Patti," published July 16, 2007, YouTube video, 3:40, https://www.youtube.com/watch?v=B9dKJWpIowc.

CHAPTER 11: A UNIQUE HUMAN BEING

1. South Dakota Codified Law 34-23A-10.1 (2005), Voluntary and Informed Consent Required—Medical Emergency Exception—Information Provided, https://sdlegislature.gov/Statutes/Codified_Laws/2057118.
2. Dr. Marcellino D'Ambrosio, Crossroads Initiative, "Mother Teresa's Letter to the US Supreme Court on Abortion and Roe v. Wade," October 1, 2016, https://www.crossroadsinitiative.com/media/articles/mother-teresas-letter -us-supreme-court-abortion-roe-v-wade/.

CHAPTER 12: MYTHS, RISKS, AND ONE LAST KISS

1. Elard Koch et al., "Women's Education Level, Maternal Health Facilities, Abortion Legislation and Maternal Deaths: A Natural Experiment in Chile from 1957 to 2007," PLOS ONE (May 4, 2012), https://journals.plos.org /plosone/article?id=10.1371/journal.pone.0036613.
2. E. G. Raymond and D. A. Grimes. "The Comparative Safety of Legal Induced Abortion and Childbirth in the US," *Obstetrics & Gynecology* 119:215–19 (2012).
3. C. Deneux-Tharaux, C. Berg, M. Boouvier-Colle, M. Gissler, M. Harper, A. Nannini, S. Alexander, K. Wildman, G. Breart, and P. Buekens. "Underreporting of Pregnancy Related Mortality in the U.S. and Europe." *Obstetrics & Gynecology* 106:684–92 (2005).
4. Mika Gissler et al., "Injury Deaths, Suicides and Homicides Associated with Pregnancy, Finland 1987-2000," *European Journal of Public Health* 15 no. 5 (October 2005): 459-63, https://academic.oup.com/eurpub/article/15/5 /459/526248.
5. For more information about risk statistics, visit AAPLOG's website at https://aaplog.org.
6. Priscilla K. Coleman, "Abortion and Mental Health: Quantitative Synthesis and Analysis of Research Published 1995-2009," *The British Journal of Psychiatry* 199, no. 3 (September 2011): 180-186, https://pubmed.ncbi.nlm .nih.gov/21881096/.
7. For more information, visit https://www.abortionpillreversal.com and https://www.heartbeatinternational.org/our-work/apr.

8. For more information on perinatal hospice, go to https://www.perinatal
hospice.org.

CHAPTER 14: IN SOLIDARITY OF LIFE

1. Oliver Wendell Holmes Sr., *The Autocrat of the Breakfast-Table*, reprint ed.
(Mineola, N.Y.: Dover Publications), 65.